M

WIT

P9-CQW-812

3 1192 01379 3664

100

to Save

and Still Ha...

Wedding

Sharon Naylor

5.22 N...
ylor,
01 w... e money-- and
ll ha... g wedding /

REVISED EDITION

McGraw·Hill

New York   Chicago   San Francisco   Lisbon   London   Madrid   Mexico City
Milan   New Delhi   San Juan   Seoul   Singapore   Sydney   Toronto

NOV 3 0 2007

EVANSTON PUBLIC LIBRARY   395.22
1703 ORRINGTON AVENUE   Naylo.5
EVANSTON, ILLINOIS 60201

Library of Congress Cataloging-in-Publication Data

Naylor, Sharon.
   1001 ways to save money . . . and still have a dazzling wedding / Sharon Naylor.—
revised ed.
      p.   cm.
   Includes index.
   ISBN 0-658-02109-5
   1. Weddings.   I. Title: One thousand one ways to save money . . . and still have
a dazzling wedding.   II. Title: One thousand and one ways to save money . . . and
still have a dazzling wedding.   III. Title.

BJ2051 .N39   2001
395.2'2—dc21   2001017359

Copyright © 2002, 1994 by Sharon Naylor. All rights reserved. Printed in the United States
of America. Except as permitted under the United States Copyright Act of 1976, no part of
this publication may be reproduced or distributed in any form or by any means, or stored
in a database or retrieval system, without the prior written permission of the publisher.

10 11 12 13 14 15 16 17 18   FGR/FGR   0 9 8 7 6

ISBN 0-658-02109-5

Cover design by Monica Baziuk
Cover illustrations by Steve Gillig

McGraw-Hill books are available at special quantity discounts to use as premiums and
sales promotions, or for use in corporate training programs. For more information, please
write to the Director of Special Sales, Professional Publishing, McGraw-Hill, Two Penn
Plaza, New York, NY 10121-2298. Or contact your local bookstore.

This book is printed on acid-free paper.

Contents

Contents

Acknowledgments

Much gratitude goes to my editor at Contemporary Books, Betsy Lancefield, who is the driving force behind this book. Additional thanks to Julia Anderson for her guidance with this edition.

My heart bursts with gratitude for the wonderful friends and brides who contributed their ideas and inspirations: Karen Beyke, Jill Althouse-Wood, Pamela Bishop, Jennifer Stinson, Susan Cefolo-McDermott, Susan DeLong, Julie Weingarden, Oksana Yurchuk, Jeanine Condon, and the many brides who attended my book-signings and lectures.

I would also like to thank Millie Somers, Annette and Ralph Corrao, Christine and George Balynsky, and the other friends and family members who took the time to be in my front row.

To all of the wonderfully helpful wedding professionals who allowed me to interview them for this book: no wonder you are the best in the business.

To Steven and Leanne, thank you for all of your help. I'm extremely proud of both of you!

And to Andrew and Joanne Blahitka, thank you for all of your support and love.

Preface

Ever since you were a young girl, you have undoubtedly imagined your wedding. You saw yourself in a beautiful white princess gown dancing with your handsome, tuxedoed husband in a grand ballroom filled with crystal chandeliers, flowers, and ice sculptures. A string quartet is playing classical selections to your five hundred guests, who sip happily at their Dom Pérignon and enjoy an eight-course meal, and then you and your husband are whisked off in a shiny, white stretch limousine for a monthlong Hawaiian honeymoon.

Every daydream produced a new addition to your lifelong vision of the perfect wedding you'd surely have. The *In Style* celebrity wedding issue inspired you to add a long train to your fantasy gown and—why not?—a ride in a horse-drawn carriage to the ceremony. Your cousin Emily's wedding, while not quite as lofty as Jennifer Aniston's, made you want the same kind of seven-tier chocolate ganache cake and an international coffee bar for your reception.

And now here you are, planning your wedding at last. You've lined up every detail of the wedding you've been dreaming of. But when you have finished the grave task of pricing everything, you find that you could purchase an airline (or at least pay off your college loans) for what it would cost to put together your big day at today's prices. Reality hits, and it'll take the wind out of any bride and groom's sails. As it seems, you'll have to either drain your life savings, cash in your savings bonds and insurance policies, sell your cars, wear protective headgear when you ask your parents for that ungodly amount of money—*or* you can start looking for ways to save money on your wedding. It seems that you've already decided on the latter. Good choice.

Money, unfortunately, is a very large part of wedding plans. The entire matrimonial industry revolves around it, in-laws squabble with the bride and groom about it, and practically every choice you'll make depends on it. But you don't have to have every aspect of your wedding controlled by a dollar sign. Instead, you can take control of the dollar sign by following the money-saving suggestions in this book. Then your ten-thousand-dollar wedding (or your five-thousand-dollar wedding or your fifty-thousand-dollar wedding) can be had for half that amount—if not less—and if you do it right, no one will be able to tell you saved any money at all.

With the help of this book, you'll learn how to have a less expensive wedding without having a cheap-looking wedding. You'll learn exactly where you should and shouldn't cut corners, how to help your family and bridal party save money, where to seek free or discounted assistance, and how to keep from feeling as if you're shortchanging yourself and your wishes just to save a few (thousand) bucks. Also included in this book are quotes from real-life brides who share how they saved (or lost) money while planning their weddings. With the money you will save, you can start your new life together in a better position financially. (And you get to keep your car!)

General Cost-Cutting Rules

A panel of real-life brides has compiled this list of general rules regarding saving money during the planning of a wedding. Keep these points in mind as you go through the rest of the book—many will apply to more than one area of your planning process.

~ Don't let the money make you crazy. There will always be a cheaper choice than the one you've made, and the bills will pile up. It's a fact of life, avoidable only through elopement. This is supposed to be an enjoyable time for you, so don't let figures and totals take away from the total wedding experience.

~ Don't let money be the main topic of conversation when you're talking to your fiancé and family about the planning. Instead of harping on and on about how much the bouquets cost, shift the focus instead to how beautiful the ceremony is going to be.

~ Don't be cheap. You must indulge in some things for yourself because you are the bride and you deserve special treatment on your wedding day. So instead of knocking out all luxuries, allow a few for yourself . . . and don't feel guilty about it.

~ Ask your friends how they saved money on their weddings. They may be able to refer you to cost-saving resources you wouldn't otherwise have found.

~ When kind relatives and friends ask to contribute their services, accept their offers. It makes them feel like a special part of your day, and it certainly helps your budget.

NEGOTIATING HELP IN LIEU OF GIFTS
Throughout this book I mention accepting your friends' and relatives' offers to help with the wedding as their gift to you. There are many places where a donation of someone's expertise or talents would not only save you money but would add a meaningful, personal touch to your big day. Here are some etiquette tips regarding accepting your loved ones' offers to help:

- Be sure they're qualified to do the job well. If your aunt offers to make your veil and she's well-known as a talented craftswoman, by all means accept her offer. If your cousin is a soloist in her church choir, you may accept her offer of a song as her wedding gift. Where it gets sticky is when someone offers to perform a task that you're not quite sure she'll be able to handle. In that case, thank her and tell her you already have someone helping with that task. Perhaps she can do something else.
- If someone offers to help, tell him that you'd be happy to accept his services as his wedding gift to you. He may refuse at first, but all it takes is a heartwarming smile and hug from you to convince him to accept your offer. It wouldn't be fair to accept free services from your guest and then expect a pricey gift as well.
- Tell your helping hand how much it means to you to have him or her contribute to your day. People love helping out for the sake of being helpful, but it's always nice to hear what the contribution means to the couple.
- Give them the spotlight at the wedding. If your aunts spent hours making baklava for the cocktail hour, ask the master of ceremonies to make an announcement and afford them a round of applause from your guests.
- Always send a thank-you card, and perhaps a little gift, after the wedding.

~ Speak up about group discounts and be daring enough to try to talk down the price. Your bravery just may earn 10 percent or so off your bill.

~ Speak up if you're not happy with an item or service. If you've ordered something and it arrives in bad condition, stand up for yourself and demand its replacement or a refund. That's a basic of good money management, not just a wedding particular.

~ Try to save money not just for yourself but for your family, the groom's family, the bridal party, and guests who will be coming to town for your wedding. Your choices do affect each of them financially, and your efforts to cut down the amounts they will have to spend will surely result in less tension and more gratitude.

~ Don't let professionals pressure you into immediate spending. Keep in mind that they may be motivated more by their 25 percent commission than by your happiness. Make the professionals wait for you to decide, so you'll have a chance to find greater savings instead of giving in to impulsive spending.

~ Don't consider the barter system beneath you. If you make a deal with your best friend that her wedding gift to you will be her performance of a song at the ceremony or doing the calligraphy for your wedding programs, then she's honored to be a part of your wedding celebration, and you've combined a special and memorable gesture with a coincidentally cost-effective plan. There's nothing shameful about that.

∽ The best parts of any wedding celebration are the personal touches added by the bride and groom: saying your own vows, singing to one another at the ceremony, decorating your reception with pictures and items that are special to the two of you. All meaning, no price.

1

Your Engagement Announcements

You can shout your good news from the rooftop for free, but it's much better to put your engagement announcement in print. Here's how to save on this portion of your wedding budget.

The Newspaper Announcement

~ Submit your announcement and picture to newspapers that do not charge for publication in their announcement column.

~ If your town's newspaper charges by the word, practice writing your announcement in the fewest words possible. One bride saved fifteen dollars just by revising and condensing.

➷ If your town's newspaper only charges a flat fee for the announcement, get your money's worth, and an even better memento, by writing a long entry filled with detail.

➷ If you'd like to put your announcement in several newspapers and they all charge printing fees, choose only the most important ones. These may be papers in your hometown, the groom's hometown, and those of both sets of parents.

➷ If you'd like to put your announcement in several papers and none of them charges a printing fee, send your article and picture to newspapers in each of the following towns: yours, the groom's, your parents', his parents', your grandparents', your old hometowns, and your college alumni newspapers.

➷ Keep in mind, though, that even though it may be free to have the article printed in the paper, you'll still have to deal with the expense of picture copies and postage. These can add up. Get inexpensive copies of your photos through photo shops, or scan them and send them to the paper via E-mail.

➷ Edit your engagement announcement well. You don't want to allow typographical errors on your part to be printed in the paper, insulting your future in-laws, whose names you've misspelled, and causing you to have to pay for an edited version of your announcement in the paper the following week.

∼ Always put your name and telephone number on the back of the picture you're submitting with the announcement. In some cases, you may be able to get the picture back for additional use or to frame.

$\int$ tationery Announcements

∼ Don't order your engagement announcements from a bridal salon or bridal shop. Those establishments are targeted specifically toward the bridal consumer, and that usually means you'll be paying top dollar.

∼ If you're ordering printed announcements of your engagement, shop around at stationery stores for the best prices. Look for special sales that can save you 10 percent, 20 percent, or more.

∼ Check www.catalog.com to order free announcement and invitation catalogs to see price comparisons, discounts, and the variety of announcement styles available.

～ Order a simple style of announcement. The price of a basic and very classy black print on white paper selection will go up if you choose a different typeface, color of print, or any additional graphics. Sometimes the savings can add up to 50 percent when you keep it simple.

～ Know exactly how many engagement announcements you'll need so you don't order too many. One bride overspent by fifty dollars (make that *wasted* fifty dollars) by ordering her announcements long before she had reached a firm number of recipients. The extra announcements now sit in a box in her closet.

～ Simply buy some high-quality paper by the pound at a discount or stationery store, and print your own announcements using a classy font on your home computer. Two excellent designed-paper sources are Paper Direct (800-A-PAPERS) and Botanical PaperWorks (888-727-3755, www.Botanical PaperWorks.com). Also, check your local Staples or OfficeMax stores for their new wedding paper and envelope lines, often found in elegant styles for four to five dollars per pack of twenty-five.

～ Either print the announcements yourself, which is the least expensive way, or take a master copy to a discount print shop and have them do it for you. Whichever you choose, the cost will still be less than if you order name-brand announcements from a catalog or specialty store.

COMPARE AND SAVE

Store-ordered announcements $80

Homemade announcements plus discount print shop ... $40

Homemade plus home-copied announcements $10

～ Perhaps the best news: if you're announcing the engagement at a party or gathering, you don't have to send out printed announcements at all. No one will miss them.

For my announcements, I raided an after-Christmas 50-percent-off sale for holiday stationery. Then I printed up announcements using my home computer and the holiday stationery, and I mailed them out the day after Christmas. They turned out lovely and perfect for the season.

—FRANCES

2

Your Engagement Party

Pop the corks and let the celebration begin! The engagement party is the kickoff of all of the once-in-a-lifetime events to come, so make this event extra special without breaking the bank.

~ Compare among store-bought engagement party invitations. The regular-sized ones are less expensive than the over-sized ones, and the simpler ones are less expensive than the decorated ones with the shiny covers and laser cutouts. Just be sure, though, that the invitation you choose reflects the level of formality of the engagement party.

~ If you're ordering your engagement party invitations from a printer, choose a simple style. A plain white invitation with black ink rather than a baby-blue one with navy ink will cost you less.

~ Make your own engagement party invitations on your home computer with a classy font and your own clip art for decoration. For further savings, search for quality paper for these homemade invitations. Your comparison shopping may find the best values at a buy-by-the-pound paper source. Again, check out Paper Direct (800-A-PAPERS), Botanical Paper-Works (888-727-3755), Staples, or OfficeMax.

~ Get your envelopes there, too. There's no need to spend extra for decorative, lined, or security envelopes.

~ Have the engagement party at home instead of at a reception hall or club. The comfortable, warm atmosphere is perfect for any level of formality.

~ If you're planning on having the engagement party catered, cut costs a bit by having only part of the meal prepared by the professionals. They make the entrée, and you make the appetizers and desserts. You can easily cut a standard caterer's bill in half.

﹏ Plan the engagement party for a time during the day when no large meal will be expected. An informal affair from 2 to 5 P.M. is adequately served with hors d'oeuvres, and a soiree starting at 7 P.M. is best served with cake and dessert.

﹏ Shop for food and supplies in bulk or at a discount supply house like Costco or Sam's Club. These places offer great party-sized packages of frozen appetizers, deli trays, fresh seafood, and desserts for far less than regular or upscale markets. Have a friend take you on her membership if you don't belong to the club.

﹏ Cut down on beverage costs by limiting the variety of alcoholic and nonalcoholic drinks, or by choosing to serve only wine and beer.

DRINKS PORTION OF CATERER'S BILL

Events *with* alcohol .... $25–$30 more
                                              per person

Events *without* alcohol .... $15 more per person

200-guest list .... $5,000–$6,000 more
                                              for alcohol

⌒ A great resource for finding affordable, high-quality vintages, plus a unique assortment of recommended beers and liquors, is www.winespectator.com. Here you'll locate the best buys for your party.

⌒ Many brides report that they saved one hundred dollars or more by having a talented friend or relative make the cake or desserts for the engagement party. Many a grandmother has "donated" her time and ingredients for chocolate mousse, homemade cannoli, exotic fruit salad, or even an expertly decorated, butter-cream-frosted cake straight out of the pages of *Martha Stewart Living*. So if your cousin makes a sinful chocolate cheesecake, ask her to bring a few along as her present to you. With engagement presents costing fifty to seventy-five dollars on the average, your cousin will secretly thank you for the giant savings. And she'll glow with pride when you announce to your guests that she is the pastry chef.

COMPARE AND SAVE

Store-bought sheet cake $45
Homemade sheet cake $20

⁓ Take your own pictures, and pass around the camera for help from family and friends. You may hire a professional photographer to take pictures at your engagement party, but you're trying to save money here, not waste it. This is just the engagement party, so informal pictures will do fine.

COMPARE AND SAVE

Professional photographer . . . . $500 and up

Do it yourself . . . . $50–$100

   (includes price of film and developing)

⁓ Instead of hiring a band, DJ, pianist, or harpist for your engagement party, turn on the stereo if the engagement party is being held in your home, or have the restaurant or reception hall pipe in appropriate music through its sound system.

COMPARE AND SAVE

Professional music . . . . $600–$800

Stereo/piped-in music . . . . free

~ As for decorations, consider a simple look. Fourteen dozen white balloons may look festive, but they're also a nonessential that can be thrown out in favor of saving some money. Create a classy look by decorating with vases of flowers cut fresh from your garden, well-placed pillar candles, or a display of photos of the two of you.

COMPARE AND SAVE

Balloons	up to $75
Vases of flowers from garden	free
Display of photos	free

~ You don't need to give out favors at the engagement party. Your guests won't expect them. But you do want to give something out—inexpensive chocolates or sachets will do the trick.

~ Of course, you may choose not to have an engagement party at all. You could make your big announcement at a family gathering such as Thanksgiving dinner and save all the fanfare for the wedding itself.

3

Getting Organized

Being organized is the number-one way to save money on your wedding. A disorganized approach can cost you extra money and time (which we all know is even more valuable than money these days).

~ Start planning and organizing early enough so that you have plenty of time to perform each job well. A rushed job means fewer chances to get more for your money. Saving money may require allowing more than a few months for the planning of your wedding and reception. Nine months to a year is optimal for finding good deals at a savings. If short-term planning is required for a wedding less than a year away, do some research to find all of your professionals and locations without paying extra rush fees. Check out my book *How to Plan an Elegant Wedding in 6 Months or Less* for time- and money-saving ideas, plus tips to keep you organized. A rush

ceremony can cost extra money, so stay on top of a challeng-
ing planning schedule.

〜 Encourage your mother or maid or matron of honor to
give you a wedding planner book as her gift to you. She'll feel
a tug of sentimentality in the gesture, and you'll save some
money at the bookstore. For discounted books and planners,
check Barnes and Noble, or Amazon.com.

BOOKS AND PLANNERS
Amazon.com—www.amazon.com
Barnes and Noble—800-242-6657, www.bn.com

〜 Use your local library's supply of wedding etiquette books
instead of buying your own. After all, when will you ever need
a wedding etiquette book again?

COMPARE AND SAVE
Bookstore wedding etiquette books . . . . $15-$30
Wedding etiquette book from library . . . . free

～ Borrow a recently married relative's or friend's wedding etiquette books.

～ Set up an organizer file using four-by-six-inch index cards and a recipe card file box. You've seen this suggested in all your bridal magazines and even in some ads for fifty-dollar index card and file-box sets with printed labels. Setting up a wedding planner file box of your own will work just as well, if not better.

～ You could also choose to turn an accordion file into your wedding organizer system. You'll find these in any office supply store for just a few dollars. Label each slot with subject headings—Gown, Flowers, Music, Caterer—and filing brochures and swatches becomes simple.

～ Use your organization system to keep track of receipts, brochures, pictures, drawings, business cards, and all the important things that can get lost. The rule goes, if you've lost it now, you'll need it later. And that can cost you money if something needs to be returned or an order needs to be placed.

～ As you've seen here, you can set up your own organization system for just pennies. Besides the fact that it's customized to your tastes and needs, it's a huge savings compared with the cost of one of those expensive computer wedding planner programs. Do you really need your computer to remind you to go for your fitting at 4 P.M.? Besides, you can't file your brochures, swatches, and store receipts in the computer's "files." While going high tech is a fun idea, it's also one of the worst cases of unnecessary wedding spending you'll ever see. Skip the software and stick with your own files, folders, or binder.

~ If you're set on having the computer help you out, use the free worksheets and tabulators at www.theknot.com or www.dellaweddings.com.

~ Aside from wedding planning website worksheets, books, and articles, get yourself on track with the use of a handheld organizer. You may already own one, so use it to create your wedding lists of to-dos, appointment reminders, and messaging centers. If you'd like to find a handheld organizer or a "palmtop" for use during the wedding planning and forever afterward, check out the following:

Casio—800-962-2746, www.casio.com

Hewlett Packard—800-724-6631, www.hp.com

Palm—800-881-7256, www.palm.com

Sharp—800-BE-SHARP, www.sharp-usa.com

WEDDING WEBSITES

The Best Man—www.thebestman.com

Bride's Magazine—www.brides.com

Della Weddings—www.dellaweddings.com

Elegant Bride—www.elegantbridemagazine.com

The Knot—www.theknot.com

Martha Stewart Living—www.marthastewart.com

Modern Bride—www.ModernBride.com

Premiere Bride—www.premierebride.com

Today's Bride—www.todaysbride.com

Ultimate Internet Wedding Guide—www.ultimate
wedding.com

Wedding Bells—www.weddingbells.com

Wedding Central—www.weddingcentral.com

The Wedding Channel—www.theweddingchannel.com

Wedding Details—www.weddingdetails.com

The Wedding Helpers—www.weddinghelpers.com

Wedding Spot—www.weddingspot.com

For quick location availability information visit www.CheckMy Date.com, plug in your wedding date and location, and this free site will list sites and vendors available on your date.

 If you cannot invest in a palmtop organizer right now, you might choose to employ one of the many *free* on-line calendars, reminder services, address books, and appointment worksheets. Some of the best are:

AOL Reminders—on America Online, go to "My AOL" and click on "Reminders"

Anyday—www.anyday.com

Visto—www.visto.com

Yahoo Calendar—www.calendar.yahoo.com

~ Let your bridal party and family members in on these organizing tools as well. Arrange to network with them to send them E-mail reminders of shopping trips, fittings, luncheons, and FYIs.

~ Always make absolutely sure that your decisions are final before you contract for services and items. This includes, of course, running your plans by the groom and by those who are helping to finance the wedding. A hastily made decision can mean money lost when a contract has to be canceled or an item returned.

~ Get everything in writing. Written records can be referred to easily for reminders and deadlines, and oral contracts will not hold up in court in case of a problem. A written record of any business agreement should include the following details for clarification: date of sale, business's name and phone number, your name and phone number, date of service, time of service, location of service, details of the service or items, delivery arrangements, payment arrangements, check number, cancellation or postponement policy, refund policy, and name and signature of the person who took the order.

Get It in Writing

Atlanta-based attorney Karen Beyke advises: "Be sure your contract has a 'time is of the essence' clause, which states that a wedding provider must deliver the items or services at the proper time on the wedding day. Too many brides have complained that the flowers showed up at the church after the ceremony, or they had to wait an hour for the cake to be delivered from the bakery. If you have this phrase in your contract, the vendor will know you mean business, and you'll be sure to get timely treatment. If the item is not delivered on time, then they are in breach of contract, and you don't have to pay."

 Also, always get a copy of any contract and confirmation numbers from the professionals who will be providing services during your ceremony or reception.

∽ Read every word of your contacts, even if you have to sit back in your chair while the impatient salesclerk rolls his or her eyes and tries to hurry you along to the check-writing stage. You never know what's hidden in the fine print—extra charges, commissions, outlandish gratuities, special conditions, waivers, and so on.

∽ If you don't understand something in the contract, don't hesitate to ask. If the clerk is throwing business jargon at you, ask for clarification.

∽ Just to be on the safe side, photocopy your contracts and keep the copies in a secure place. In case of loss, theft, or fire, you're still on secure ground with the larger expenses of your wedding. Don't hire anyone who won't give you a copy of the contract.

∽ Get receipts for each of your deposits, signed and dated by the salesclerk. This way, you're preventing the old you–never–paid-me trick that some shadier companies might try on you.

∽ If you do wind up with a problem, go straight to the manager. No boss wants his or her business to get a bad report from an unhappy customer. Wedding industry professionals know that much of their business comes from referrals, and a bad reputation can slow down the flow of customers. The manager, you'll find, will be quick to fix the problems. If not, go to consumer action groups and consumer action columns in your local paper (that'll get them hopping to please you), the Better Business Bureau if you fear for those who will come after you, and the professional association affiliated with the business itself. To find your local chapter of the Better Business Bureau, log on to their site at www.bbb.org for company search instructions and report information. To check out an Internet company, contact the Better Business Bureau's OnLine Reliability program at www.bbbonline.org. These sites will assist in background searches on various companies you may be considering as vendors.

∼ Keep lists so you don't forget anything. Follow the lists provided in wedding books and magazines, or make up your own. (Ask the groom, the bridal party, and your families to do the same.)

∼ Keep several pads and pencils around the house, in your car, and at the office for when a thought or a question strikes you. Another rule of the wedding planner: if you think you'll remember it later, you won't. Write it down.

∼ Keep a mini tape recorder or handheld organizer, if you have one, in your purse or car for the same reason.

~ One of your most important lists should be a price comparison list. Accounting ledgers are good for this job. You'll be able to assign each caterer, photographer, or band its own column, where you'll record prices and package details. Use this setup as you price all the services you'll need. A quick glance down a column on one piece of paper will reveal the choice with the best price and the most attractive offerings for that price. One bride who used this system found that she was better able to compare all the different packages, and in picking the best one she saved three hundred fifty dollars.

~ Keep a master list of phone numbers so you don't have to keep looking up important numbers or calling information. Each call to your phone company's directory number can cost you several dollars.

~ Record upcoming deadlines on both your home and work calendars, and record what you've already done as well. You may need to know exactly what day you ordered your gown so the salesperson can tell you if yours has arrived in the latest shipment.

~ For each service you're arranging, call to confirm your order, delivery, and prices several times throughout the wedding planning months. You never can be too sure.

∼ Send confirmation letters, and keep copies for yourself, both as proof and as reminders of each step in the process. E-mail is good for this, and it's free.

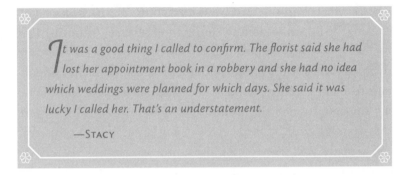

It was a good thing I called to confirm. The florist said she had lost her appointment book in a robbery and she had no idea which weddings were planned for which days. She said it was lucky I called her. That's an understatement.

—STACY

∼ Keep samples of fabric, ribbon, and lace and pictures of your gown and reception site in a box in your car so that you'll always have access to them when you're out shopping, at a big fabric sale, or in another city. Never guess at the color of your bridesmaids' dresses when you're out to buy coordinating items. A clash is a waste of money and shows your guests that you were unorganized and trying too hard to save some money.

∼ Keep track of every wedding response you receive. Your final head count depends on those numbers, and it is that figure that tallies up one of the biggest expenses of your wedding:

the catering. Keep your responses and a working yea-and-nay list in a large envelope or in your organizer, bound with a rubber band.

∾ Do you really need a wedding coordinator to keep you organized? Some women swear by their services, claiming that the organizer was responsible for putting together a wedding that couldn't possibly have been more perfect. While it's important to recognize the value of a coordinator to someone who has no time to plan the wedding or is too distant from where the wedding will be held (cases in which hiring an organizer can actually save money), it's also a money-saving fact that you can coordinate your wedding yourself. It takes time and a lot of footwork, but most brides say that's the best part of planning the wedding. Handing this job over to a stranger—and paying hundreds if not thousands of dollars for it—just may not make sense to you.

∾ If you *need* a wedding consultant—either because you're much too busy to call thirty bakeries for prices or because you're several states away from where the wedding will be held—be sure the consultant you choose is a good one. Ask for references.

∾ Ask a recently married friend to recommend the consultant she used.

∽ Make sure the consultant is a member of the Association of Bridal Consultants (860-355-0464). Considering how much you'll be paying, it's best to make sure the person you hire is legitimate and well trained.

∽ Times have changed in the wedding coordination business. You are not limited to the usual coordinator-does-everything contract, as there are now several options to fit your personal style and budget. Shirley Feuerstein of Affairs and Arrangements in New Jersey says that wedding coordinators now offer several types of packages. The all-inclusive packages, where the coordinators do all the planning, are the most commonly known, but a good planner will also offer the option of hiring him or her just for the search and selection of vendors or just as ringleader for the wedding day. These options often save the bride and groom time and a lot of money. Check with your prospective coordinators to see what kinds of packages are available to you.

∽ When you hire a wedding consultant, carefully review the guidelines set up for your business relationship. Make sure you're both clear where your responsibilities begin and end, and don't hesitate to ask questions. It's *your* wedding.

A common situation facing more and more brides today is the problem of distance. Maybe it's because we're traveling more, meeting our men in places that bring people from distant parts together, and computers make it easier to carry on serious long-distance relationships. Whatever the reason, you'll still have to keep in contact with his and your families and friends who may be miles away during the planning stages of the wedding. Long-distance communication can cost money— a whole lot of it—so follow these steps for better, more-economical distance organization.

~ Know your phone company's off-rate hours and call then to save money on each call. At economy rates, the price per minute for your call could be half the regular rate. That translates into cutting your phone bills by 50 percent, and some brides have saved up to two hundred dollars.

~ Send E-mails regularly, updating on changes and decisions, asking for help or advice, and thanking everyone for his or her cooperation up to that point. The advantage of E-mails: you can send links to your bridesmaids so they can see the gown, their dresses, shoes, and so on. Plus, copying several people at once makes the job fast and easy.

~ Use postcards for short messages such as arrival dates, rehearsal times, fitting dates, and so on.

~ Send a copy of the wedding schedule to each member of the bridal party and to the families and friends who will be taking part in the wedding. This way, everyone is sure about what days to keep clear far in advance. Dates and times will not have to be shuffled.

～ Have the bridesmaids, maid or matron of honor, best man, and ushers send you their measurements and sizes on index cards. With this information, you won't have to phone around to get them to admit their sizes when it's time to order their apparel. If shyness is a problem, have them send you their index cards in sealed envelopes to be opened only by the salesperson at the shop.

～ Tell your attendants to have their sizes measured at a professional tailor's or seamstress's workshop; measurements taken with a tape measure or a piece of string and a ruler aren't nearly as legitimate. One bridesmaid who took her own measurements with a tape measure misread her hip measurement and ordered the wrong size dress. When it arrived, it didn't fit, and she had to buy another dress on the double.

～ To help your attendants and families stay organized—and to keep them from calling you all the time for one another's phone numbers—send out phone and address lists of all the key players.

∼ Keep everyone up to date on all the plans that have been made. This includes your families, the bridal party, the parents of child attendants, and those who will be taking part in the ceremony as readers, performers, or guest registrars.

∼ If a bridal party or family member is slow in responding with important information, don't hesitate to explain how important it is to stay with the schedule. Apply some gentle pressure to get the job done. Or just use the broken record approach. Call the person up and say, "I don't remember if I've asked you this, but did you send me your size card already?" Of course, you know she didn't, but it doesn't hurt to play forgetful to get your point across.

4

Finding Savings
at Bridal Shows

More than just a showcase of the talent available in your area, free drinks, and appetizers, the bridal show can lead you to extra discounts and even free honeymoons, gowns, and wedding day beauty treatments! Find out here how to make the most of your visits to bridal shows.

~ Go to the bridal show to collect brochures, business cards, and prices (if they're available at the show) for your research. No need to travel all over town to all the bridal shops, shoe stores, caterers, florists, and photographers if each has information set up and available at the bridal show.

BRIDAL ASSOCIATION RESOURCES

Bridal Shows and Conferences
Great Bridal Expo—800-422-3976, www.bridalexpo.com

Limousines
National Limousine Association—800-NLA-7007

Organizations
Association of Bridal Consultants—860-355-0464
American Federation of Musicians—212-869-1330
American Society of Travel Agents—703-739-2782,
   www.astanet.com
Better Business Bureau—www.bbb.org (to find the Better
   Business Bureau in your state or locale)
Professional Photographers of America—800-786-6277,
   www.ppa-world.org

∼ Just use the show to get a sense of what you want from a three-dimensional representation of what you see in bridal magazines.

∼ Some businesses set up at the bridal show may offer discounts to those brides who sign up for their services on the spot. This takes away from your ability to comparison shop, so it may not be a good idea to go for the offer right away. Take time to check before you commit. You can always take their card and call them.

〜 Door prizes are awarded at most bridal shows. They can range from silver frames to gift certificates for a wedding day makeover. Sign up for all giveaways. At a recent bridal show, one bride won a six-thousand-dollar Hawaiian honeymoon package and another won six free tuxedo rentals. Not bad for a twenty-dollar entrance fee. Any gift is money in your pocket.

〜 Speaking of gifts, you'll find samples of every kind at bridal shows. Makeup, perfumes, little portions of cake—all offered there for you to try without expense or obligation. So take advantage of these.

〜 While you're there, see if there are any mailing lists you'd like to get on. Perhaps you'll be offered discounts. Just be prepared later for an onslaught of mail. The list you sign and the information you give may be sold to other retailers and businesses looking to attract your checkbook. For information on dates and times for bridal shows scheduled for your area, call 800-422-3976 for the Great Bridal Expo; Macy's stores across the nation hold regular bridal events, as well, as does The Knot at www.theknot.com.

WEDDING ITEM RESOURCES

Check these websites if you are looking for wedding items such as toasting flutes, ring pillows, and so on.

Affectionately Yours—www.affectionately-yours.com

Beverly Clark Collection—877-862-3933,
    www.beverlyclark.com

Bridalink Store—www.bridalink.com/store2

Chandler's Candle Company—800-463-7143,
    www.chandlerscandle.com

Magical Beginnings Butterfly Farms—888-639-9995,
    www.butterflyevents.com (live butterflies for release)

The Sarina Collection—888-6SARINA,
    www.sarinacollection.com

The Wedding Shopper—
    www.theweddingshopper.com/catalog.htm

Treasured Moments—800-754-5151,
    www.treasured-moments.com

~ Take the groom along with you so that he can check out all of the wedding planning options. Having him there saves time and money, as you won't miss out on offers because he's not around to share in the decision. If he needs a little prodding to attend one of these shows, just tell him there's free food, drinks, and entertainment.

~ Play the games. The more creative vendors at the bridal event will have "try-your-luck" games such as a wheel of discounts that you can spin to win percentages off their services or merchandise. Of course, these winnings are to be used only as incentives, not as your decision to hire that particular vendor. If it checks out well during your comparison shopping, that 25-percent-off coupon will come in handy.

~ Participate in the show. Bridal shows often have mingling time during which you look at the booths. They also have an entertainment portion of the night when bands and DJs give performances to an admiring (and checkbook-holding) audience. If a DJ asks for a volunteer to come up on stage, either to take part in a conga line or simply sit there and be serenaded, you may want to raise your hand. Very often participants get a free gift or discount coupon.

~ Talk to the experts to get ideas on how to save. While trying to win your booking the pros will be very happy to chat with you as you ask about budget-cutting particulars for your wedding. For instance, a videographer may tell you more about editing costs, special effects fees, and efficient scheduling for the wedding day.

~ Stay until the end of the night. When the crowd clears out, some vendors make a practice of giving away their props to bridal-show attendees, rather than throwing them out. You might walk away with makeup samples, favors, chocolates, even lovely silk centerpieces that can add to your wedding day decor. One bride shared that the free silk centerpieces she got from a tired vendor made great decorations for the reception hall's rest rooms. If she had ordered those from her florist she would have paid two hundred fifty dollars for live arrangements.

~ Check the parking lot before you leave. Often the transportation companies bring a limousine, a stretch Navigator, even their decked-out party buses for prospective brides and grooms to see. One bride stepped into the party bus of a limousine company, heard the great sound system, saw the mood lighting and comfortable leather seats, and, after comparing costs for four limos for her bridal party, decided on the better buy—and the incredibly fun ride—of the party bus instead.

5

Your Bridal Registry

You can save money by registering at the right places, at the right times, and for the right items. Too many brides cost themselves a big chunk of their gift money by leaving important items off their registry lists, having to buy necessities later. Here are the best ways to create your lists, plus some great registry sources.

⌁ Meet with the bridal registry consultant before you begin filling out your choices. She'll be able to answer your questions, direct you to resources you wouldn't have known about otherwise, and tell you about special messages and directions you can add to your registry file. Karen and Greg added this message to their registry file: "We prefer simple and elegant styles rather than busy or patterned styles." They received all appropriate items and saved themselves the hassle and expense of exchanges.

∿ Obviously, it's smarter to register for things you need—like blankets, a coffeemaker, a microwave oven—than to fill your dream sheet with all those fun little extras and gadgets such as a shampoo dispenser for the shower or a personalized doormat. The idea is for the guests to help you set up your household, not to fill it with junk you'll have to clear out of the way for the new microwave you had to buy with your wedding money.

∿ If you're going to register for things you need, why not register at a place other than the local china and crystal store? Home Depot has a popular registry system set up, and many brides and grooms prefer receiving tools and household appliances they really need. Check out different kinds of stores aside from the usual department and convenience stores.

∿ Register for items in a wide range of expenses so that guests of all income levels have choices they can afford. Great ideas for inexpensive gifts include wines, books, CDs, kitchen gadgets, linens, and other items under twenty-five dollars.

∿ Print "gift certificates welcome" on your bridal registry account so guests know they can take the pressure out of choosing a present for you by getting a certificate to one of your favorite stores. Just be sure to list which stores you prefer. Many couples love getting gift certificates because they can buy the items that weren't chosen on their registry, they can pool twenty gift certificates to the same department store to buy the big-ticket item that no guest could afford, and they get a fun, guilt-free shopping spree.

∽ Let the maid or matron of honor and best man know what your much-wanted big-ticket item is, such as a home entertainment center, new computer, scanner, or mountain bikes. Your top attendants can consider pooling resources with the rest of the bridal party to get you an expensive item as their group wedding gift to you. This works as well with your parents. One couple expressed an interest in adding a room to their house, and the parents of the bride and groom joined forces to give them a check for that construction project as their wedding gift.

∽ Check out honeymoon and mortgage registries. Set up an account for a honeymoon fund and tell the honor attendants about the option of guests contributing to that fund. Some banks set up mortgage registries, so check with your bank about that option as well. Warning: it is never appropriate to ask for money as a wedding present, so you're going to have to be subtle about this kind of registry. No E-mails alerting guests to this fund, no wire transfer notices, no "please give" postcards. This kind of registry is still etiquette-sensitive, so have your honor attendants spread the word verbally.

⌒ Consult the following wedding registries list for your selection of where to register. Of course, many more registries are out there, and you'll find them listed in the *Bridal Registry Book* by Leah Ingram (Contemporary Books).

> *Bed Bath & Beyond*—800-GO-BEYOND, www.bedbathandbeyond.com
>
> *Bloomingdales*—800-888-2WED, www.bloomingdales.com
>
> *Crate and Barrel*—800-967-6696
>
> *Della Weddings*—www.dellaweddings.com
>
> *Dillards*—800-626-6001, www.dillards.com
>
> *Eddie Bauer Home Collection*—800-645-7467
>
> *Fortunoff*—800-937-4376
>
> *The Gift*—www.thegift.com
>
> *Gift Emporia.com*—www.giftemporia.com
>
> *Home Depot*—www.homedepot.com
>
> *Linens N' Things*—800-568-8765

Macy's Wedding Channel—888-92-BRIDES,
www.macys.weddingchannel.com

Marshall Field's—800-243-6436

National Bridal Service—www.weddingexperts.com/nbs

Neiman Marcus—www.neimanmarcus.com

Pier 1 Imports—800-245-4595, www.pier1.com

Sears—www.sears.com

Service Merchandise—800-251-1212,
www.servicemerchandise.com

Target's Club Wedd Gift Registry—800-888-9333,
www.target.com

The Wedding List—800-345-7795,
www.theweddinglist.com

Wedding Network (Internet wedding registry)—
800-628-5113, www.weddingnetwork.com

Williams Sonoma—800-541-2376, www.williams
-sonoma.com

〜 If you're getting married at an older age, after you already
have a fully stocked home and really don't want gifts, save your
guests some money by asking them to donate their resources or
time to their favorite charities in lieu of giving wedding presents to you.

~ Make it easy on your guests. Have your honor attendants spread the word that you're registered at a store that has an on-line registry. (Some offer free shipping as well.) Your less computer-savvy guests may not be interested in such high-tech options, but a great many others will appreciate the ease of on-line shopping.

~ Let your friends and family know by word of mouth where you're registered so that you know you'll be getting exactly what you want. (It's considered rude to print your registry information in a wedding invitation.)

~ Be sure to have your address printed at the top of the registry file so that guests who are unable to attend your wedding will know where to send their gifts.

~ When you're writing down which toaster, wok, and pressure cooker you'd like, be sure to include the model numbers of the items, so that you will receive exactly what you want.

~ If the registry form doesn't have a space for them, enter the color themes of each room of your house in the "extras" section. That way, you'll eliminate the problem of "Nice quilt, but it clashes with our colors."

～ After you hand in your registry checklist, plan to get a printout of your registry as soon as it's entered into the computer. Search for and correct mistakes in your file right away.

～ Plan to update your registry after your engagement party, bridal showers, your own shopping trips throughout the months of planning, or whenever gifts are received to prevent your receiving duplicates.

～ Sorry, but you can't register for cash. You can't tell your guests to give you cash instead of a present. Many brides have asked me about the etiquette rules for cash gifts, and I'm sorry to report that your guests will have to make up their own minds as to whether or not to give you a check. Do not rationalize that if you do not register, then your guests will automatically give you cash gifts. What you're more likely to get is the guest's idea of the perfect present, which could be his-and-hers, cow-shaped milk dispensers for morning coffee. (Don't laugh; it has happened.)

～ After your wedding, get a printout of your registry so you'll have a record of the things you wanted but didn't receive. It's a ready-made birthday, anniversary, and Christmas gift list.

6

Your Bridal Party

Before you bestow the honors upon your closest friends and relatives, read this chapter for budget issues that arise in selecting your bridal party. Don't forget that being an honor attendant will cost your chosen few a pretty penny, so look for ways to help them save cash as well.

⌁ Choose a smaller bridal party, perhaps limited to sisters and brothers. After all, if you have eight bridesmaids and eight ushers plus flower girls and ring bearers, you'll have to pay for that many gifts, perhaps arrange lodging for all of them, rent more limos, and so on. Not only is a smaller bridal party a savings for you, it will also prevent headaches over which of your cousins, friends, and coworkers to include in the lineup. One bride estimated her expenses per attendant—including gifts, planning luncheons, and apparel (her choice)—to be one hundred seventy-five dollars. Others estimated their per-attendant amount in the fifty-to-seventy-five-dollar range.

∼ Consider just having a maid or matron of honor and a best man as your bridal party. Male relatives can act as ushers to seat the guests.

∼ Just have flower girls. It's a charming look. Beverly was able to outfit and buy gifts for her six flower girls for the cost of one designer-style bridesmaid's dress.

∼ Rather than having to choose a few friends out of a handful of special ones, choose none. The same goes for your twelve first cousins. It sounds harsh, but you can explain that you love them all and didn't want to leave anyone out.

∼ When you choose your bridal party, particularly the maid or matron of honor and best man, be sure you can depend on the people you're involving. Maturity and dependability are important. You don't want to include disinterested people who aren't able to keep appointments and deadlines because a big party just came up or something really good was on television. Remember, your bridal party is more than just a collection of well-dressed men and women; the position has meaning and purpose. You don't want to have to spend your time and money backtracking on the responsibilities of your attendants.

~ Don't be pressured to choose people based on their standing in the family in general (such as all cousins). Your honor attendants should be individually special to you.

~ Don't include obviously bitter, jealous, or unsupportive attendants or ushers out of a sense of responsibility. These people will be impossible to work with, and they'll put a damper on your day.

~ Don't include someone just because you were in her bridal party years ago. You should *not* use your wedding to "pay back" people.

~ The best way to save money on your bridal party is to keep them updated on your decisions, supply them with lists of their responsibilities and deadlines, and be receptive to their input throughout. People management is a smart way to save yourself extra trouble and expense.

~ Don't offer to pay for their wardrobe or travel. Some well-meaning brides make the grand gesture, which is wonderful if you have an endless budget. But making a big offer like this can lead to big expenses.

~ If your bridal party is traveling into town for the wedding, save a few bucks by getting them all one or two hotel rooms, rather than individual rooms for each couple. You can easily fit two couples into one standard room with double beds. Think twice about letting bridal party members stay at your place unless you truly do have extra bedrooms. You'll have a lot to do during the days before the wedding and you won't want to entertain houseguests when you're supposed to be focused on the wedding.

~ Try to find ways to save them money. Tell them to E-mail rather than call long-distance. Choose inexpensive designers for their gowns and tuxes. Give them their accessories as gifts. Hint that you'd prefer a more casual shower, not high tea at a fancy hotel. Let them know that you care about their expenses and that you don't want to burden them with exorbitant price tags. I hear too many stories about bitter bridesmaids who resent the bride for being too self-focused and demanding with expenses. Your bridal party should enjoy this time, not dread every phone call from you about another fifty dollars they have to shell out.

7

Setting a Budget

I know, I know. Setting a budget is about as much fun as serving jury duty, but it's a vital part of planning a wedding efficiently and frugally than you might without a plan. It's important to keep in mind that a budget can be adjusted during the course of your planning to reflect your true wants and needs, so you don't have to begin this task with dread. Many brides I've spoken to report that they loved beating the numbers in their budgets by finding great deals and shifting the extra money into other areas of their wedding expenses. Learn here how to create a workable budget for the wedding of your dreams.

~ Before you sit down to create your wedding budget, research the prices of basic wedding services in your area. That way, your budget will be more realistic.

~ List every single expense you will have to face. Start with the obvious ones, then look through magazines and ask married friends about all those hidden extras. To cheer yourself up, list what you can get for free.

~ Then make another list of the top three or four things on which you'll spare no expense—or at least not scrimp on too much. These may be your gown, the catering, your honeymoon—whatever you feel most strongly about. With these items arranged, you'll be better able to find the right places to cut spending.

~ Add to your list of expenses a reserve for any miscellaneous spending that may come up, such as taxes, tips, and transport fees, so you won't chip away at the main budget with all the little things.

~ Look at your available cash flow to see where you stand. Designate a percentage of your savings and projected income until the wedding date to determine your wedding funds. You don't want to throw yourself far into debt with loans or a drain on your credit cards, and you don't want to sell your prized possessions to dig yourself out of the hole after the big day. Don't plan to spend the amount you expect in wedding checks. It's better to stick with what you have than to overextend yourselves.

~ Decide how the expenses will be divided. What will your parents be able and willing to finance? The groom's parents? What will you foot the bill for? This list will take some work, as money can be a highly sensitive issue to everyone involved in planning a wedding. Foster a sense of cooperation and compromise. Full input by all is recommended so that no one feels as if they've been unfairly assigned an expenditure. The result will be a smart outline for the handling of your wedding budget.

~ Try to save money for everyone involved. Bear in mind your families' and friends' cash flows when you make decisions that will affect them, and they in turn will try to help save money for you as well.

~ Be sensitive if one family is in a higher income bracket than the other. It's unfair to burden one with the job of keeping up with the other. Keep expenses for both groups even so neither family feels it is doing more than the other. Nothing fosters family tensions faster than money problems.

~ Don't push expenses off onto your families. Not only is it inconsiderate to ask too much, you could be handing over a certain amount of control over your decisions as well. What bride hasn't heard, "I'm paying for this, aren't I?"

~ Keep a working record of your expenses as you go along. It's best to keep on top of the flow of checks and bills.

~ Use a computer finance program such as Quicken or Microsoft Money to keep track of your wedding expenses. These programs will categorize your expenses, let you know what the totals are in each category, alert you to bill due dates, and help keep you on budget by giving you a clear, organized picture of the checks you're writing and the charges you're making. Most standard computers come with these programs, so don't spend extra on them.

~ Don't become a slave to the magic number. Your budget is just a framework to keep your spending under control. If the flowers actually cost you sixty-five dollars more than you'd expected, don't cut the grandmothers' corsages just to slide under the limit. Most brides believe they lost control of their spending (not to mention their temper) when they felt most constrained by the budget they'd arranged months ago. They ignored the unrealistic numbers in their own budgets.

~ If you think the budget might turn into additional pressure for you (perhaps you've had experience with budgeting before), set your limits slightly higher than you'd like them to be. An extra twenty dollars tacked onto each projected expenditure could make you feel triumphant instead of guilty when you sign the photographer's contract for five dollars under your budget. (Sure, it's a game you play with yourself, but it's important to downplay the significance of the money so that you don't start to feel it's controlling your wedding.)

~ Know the difference between price and value. Always think of what you're getting in terms of quality. Never, ever choose the least expensive option because you'll always be disappointed. Find a happy medium between price and product and make your decisions based on value.

~ Price items and services on the Internet and through in-store research to get a good idea of the going rates *before* you set your budget. Don't guess and don't simply ask others what they paid for their flowers. Send for free brochures, call for price lists, look at vendor guides on the supermarket shelf and in bookstores. Creating a realistic budget using the current numbers in the market is the best way to save money in the long run.

~ Talk to a wedding consultant for a free initial consultation to see if he or she can help shave money from your budget.

~ Practice your bargaining skills. I always advise brides and grooms to try to negotiate discounts and free items on volume purchases. Negotiation takes a little practice and a lot of self-confidence, but it's the best way to get the most for your money. It sounds odd, but try your luck at a flea market in town. That's where real haggling takes place, and you may perfect your skills before trying your hand at the wedding vendors.

～ If you do arrange a service for well below the amount you originally budgeted for it, exercise great control by not blowing the amount you saved on something trivial. Instead, enter that amount in a reserve that will allow you to slip slightly over budget in another category . . . like your gown.

～ Lower the number of guests if you need to cut expenses. Just don't try this after the invitations have been sent. You can't uninvite a person.

～ Lower the formality of the wedding if your introductory research indicates that a formal dinner reception will be too expensive. Choose an alternative that is more economical, such as a luncheon or a tea party.

> **CATERER'S PRICES**
>
> Full dinner for fifty .... $100–$150 per guest
>
> Luncheon for fifty .... $60–$90 per guest
>
> Tea party for fifty .... $40–$50 per guest

∼ Try the age-old barter system. See if you can trade your professional services for free or discounted vendor contracts. In many cases you might be able to talk the vendor into giving you a percentage off services in exchange for an hour of your time as a professional office organizer or as an artist who can stencil a border in his or her shop.

∼ What about getting services for free in exchange for advertising the vendor's product? Much has been written about this new practice in the wedding industry, with some couples even going on television to rave about how they got their entire weddings for free by emblazoning their wedding programs with such notations as "flowers provided by . . . ." While you might be able to arrange for such free services, be smart about your choices and don't turn your wedding into the Super Bowl. We're attacked by advertising twenty-four hours a day, and your guests may find it tacky to have business cards and media kits at their table place settings. Choose wisely and advertise subtly if you use this tactic. Perhaps your florist will allow you to simply set a pretty box of their business cards next to a floral arrangement in the reception hall's main room.

∽ Another way to trim the budget is to ask friends and relatives how they might be able to help you out. Borrowing and free services are the best ways to save money on your wedding. This will be discussed more throughout the book.

8

The Season and Date of Your Wedding

Timing is everything, and the thirty-two-billion-dollar wedding industry puts a price tag on all of its offerings according to supply and demand at certain times of the year. Choosing the right date for your wedding could save you a bundle!

⌇ First, allow yourself plenty of time to consider several seasons for your wedding. This might mean up to a year of waiting and planning, but you can save a lot of money with careful research in this area.

⌇ Ask about seasonal charges for the ceremony and reception locations. Again, busier wedding months may mean the manager has increased package rates.

~ The most popular months for weddings (and therefore the months where supply and demand sometimes mean that prices will be higher) are June, August, and September, with May, July, October, and December following closely behind. So, for the best availability and rates—and according to some brides, better service from unhurried vendors—consider planning your wedding during January through April or in November. Of course, always compare prices for any date you choose. With the right selections, you may be able to put together an inexpensive fete smack in the middle of June.

~ Reconsider a Saturday-night gala event. It is still pretty much the norm for brides and grooms to have their weddings on a Saturday, so that is the day of the week that is most highly booked and most expensive. The trend now is to hold Friday-night weddings or Sunday-afternoon weddings. These alternative days are less expensive, more easily booked, and offer great alternatives to the standard Saturday-night sit-down dinner at one hundred fifty dollars a head. A late Friday-night reception may be a champagne and dessert event at 9 P.M., or a Sunday-afternoon event may be an outdoor wedding on the beach. So consider it now while the wedding industry still considers these days "off days" and does not charge more for them. As time goes by, they will become standard, and there will be no price difference.

~ The season of your wedding also determines if you'll have weather factors to consider. Are you planning an outdoor wedding during the rainy season? If so, when you have to move everyone and everything indoors, the garden tea party that was much less expensive than a sit-down dinner will wind up costing you much more than you had planned.

WEATHER SERVICE

For checking the weather at your ceremony, reception, or honeymoon site, including five-day forecasts and weather bulletins

AccuWeather—www.accuweather.com
Sunset Time—(precise sunset time for any day of the year)
    www.usno.navy.mil
Weather Channel—www.weather.com

~ Will it be the stormy time of year where you're planning to spend your honeymoon? A great deal of money will be wasted if you lose a day or two of your vacation because a flight was delayed by a hurricane. So consider the seasonal weather when you plan your wedding and honeymoon.

∽ The travel industry is also controlled by seasonal rates. Off-season airfare and hotel reservations can amount to hundreds of dollars' savings over high-season tourist prices. Check with your travel agent about seasonal travel prices when you begin your planning, or check directly with airlines, hotels, and tourism boards.

∽ Holidays also affect the price of travel for the bride and groom and for family and friends who will come from miles away to share your day with you. Either travel and lodging fees will soar skyward due to holiday visiting, or special holiday travel packages may be offered to lure customers away from competitors. Research holiday travel rates thoroughly before you plunk down a few thousand on Memorial Day weekend. You might be able to get a better deal at another time.

∽ Another way to facilitate travel: plan your wedding for the weekend of a family gathering or reunion. Everyone will be in the general area, and they'll get two great events for one trip. One bride found that when she moved her wedding date to an earlier weekend, more of her guests would be in the area after a family party, and she saved over a thousand dollars in travel and lodging for her guests.

∽ The season of your wedding will also affect the price of the flowers you choose for your bouquets and decorations.

Blooms and plants are usually cheaper when they're in season, so consider your florist bill when you set a date. Furthermore, a wedding planned for Valentine's Day faces an increased charge for much-in-demand roses. Sixty-dollar bouquets on Valentine's Day go for less than twenty dollars the day after, so imagine what your wedding flowers will cost.

~ Prices and types of food on the wedding menu will also be affected by the season. Warmer days mean lighter, simpler foods, and certain types of seafood are less expensive when in season.

WEDDING DATES TO AVOID

To avoid high prices, stay away from the popular holiday wedding dates, such as New Year's Eve and Valentine's Day. For all the glory of sentimentality, you'll pay a very high price.

One bride confides that you also should not plan your wedding too close to tax season, around April fifteenth and shortly thereafter. "Everyone was so stressed out about the taxes they owed, they couldn't travel or give us the kinds of gifts they would have otherwise been able to give," she says. So if you're in a high tax bracket, skip the middle of April.

9

The Time of Day

The clock decides not only the formality of your event but also the expenses that go along with it. Use this chapter to decide if you and your fiancé are going to be morning people or night people.

~ For their own reasons, some wedding sites charge different rates for different times of the day, so it may be less expensive to have the ceremony in the morning than in the afternoon or evening. When researching ceremony locations, look through price brochures or ask questions to find out if your choice has a time factor in the fees.

~ According to wedding tradition and etiquette standards, the time of day of the wedding and reception determines the degree of formality. A morning wedding and brunch will cost

nowhere near the total for the ultraformal candlelight ceremony and 8 P.M. sit-down dinner affair. So when choosing a
time to reserve the ceremony site and reception hall, consider
the festivities appropriate to that time of day.

~ Beyond formality, it's simply less expensive to serve your
guests a wonderful range of hors d'oeuvres at 1 P.M. than filet
mignon at 9 P.M. Plan your menu according to time of day for
greater savings. Done properly, offering hors d'oeuvres can be
every bit as classy as the full-meal arrangement. More so, perhaps, depending on your choices and presentation.

~ Another plus for the earlier reception: it's easier to get
away with having an economical nonalcoholic reception earlier
in the afternoon than it is at night.

~ Consider the weather. If you plan an outdoor wedding
for the hottest part of the day, your roses will wilt and your
cake may slide off the table. It has happened. The weather
becomes a factor in your expenses, or—more likely—in wasted
expenses on the big day. Check out the average weather conditions for your wedding date and time and make your decisions accordingly.

∼ The time of day may affect traffic patterns in your area and on the roads leading to your area. Arrival times for guests, the officiant, your flowers, your cake, and even yourself may be affected if major logjams occur on the highways near your site. This is especially true if you've planned your wedding for a holiday weekend. Rather than allowing the traffic to adversely affect your day, you can save money in wasted fees and delays by figuring travel times into your delivery and travel schedules.

∼ Be careful of extra charges related to the time of day of your wedding. Some locations and companies will charge you extra for a late-night wedding if they cannot get in to clean up or break down items until the next morning. That means an extra day's rental fees. An earlier wedding means your guests will be gone by 7 or 8 P.M., and the items can be returned on the same day.

∼ Think of your guests' schedules. A Friday-night wedding scheduled to start at 6 P.M. may mean that many of your guests will not be able to get to the ceremony or the cocktail hour in time because of their work schedules and travel times. Even if they don't show up until well into the reception, you've still paid their per-head fees for the cocktail hour. The best way to avoid such wasted money is to have a Friday-night wedding at 8 P.M. (which makes it a formal event) or have a Sunday event at 3 P.M. (allowing for church availability times after services) or 12 P.M. if it's a nonchurch wedding.

 An earlier ceremony and reception also means you'll have plenty of time in the evening to set off on your honeymoon. You'll save money this way by not having to pay seventy-five dollars for a post-reception hotel room the night before an early flight.

10

Your Wedding Location

Where you hold your wedding is almost as important financially as the type of wedding you plan. Certain locations obviously cost more, but some bring extra expenses you may not be aware of. Use this chapter to select the most cost-efficient location for your big event and to find ways to save once you book it.

~ Of course, your church or synagogue may be the obvious choice for reasons other than the minimal expense of reserving it for your ceremony. Most establishments just ask for a donation and an officiant's fee, and that is still much better than a five-hundred-dollar location rental bill.

~ Meet with your officiant about scheduling and restrictions. Before you make any plans or put down any deposits, you'll need to know if there are rules about which musical selections and performers you can arrange and whether or not photographers are allowed. If, for instance, you find that your church does not allow harp music during wedding ceremonies, you will lose the deposit you already gave to the harpist.

☞ Be up-front about any special information the officiant should know. Attempting to hide such things as your different religions is a very bad idea. You could find your ceremony canceled on you if your officiant is strict about limits.

Your Search for a Wedding Location

☞ Look around far in advance. Most churches and synagogues are booked up to a year or two in advance. Looking early can get you in the door or give you a head start in looking for alternate locations.

☞ Use a place with which you are familiar.

☞ Make sure the location is suitable for your religions. Some religious officiants will not conduct rites in certain secular locations. Ask the officiant to review the site and give you *written* approval for it.

◠ Make sure the location is suitable for the number of guests who will be attending your ceremony. A chapel that's too large will make your wedding look barely attended. A setting that's too small will cause grumbling over standing-room-only or too-hot conditions.

◠ Make sure the location offers the necessary facilities: rest rooms, electricity, parking, handicapped access, and so on.

◠ Will it be necessary to rent chairs and other items in order to use this location for the ceremony? It could turn out to be an expensive proposition, as chair rentals can reach into the hundreds of dollars. It's best to book a site that offers comfortable and adequate seating.

◠ Make sure you will be allowed enough time in that location for the completion of your ceremony. You don't want to be rushed out of the place so the next wedding can begin.

◠ Does this location match the formality of your wedding?

◠ Will your deposit be returned if you decide against this location?

∿ If you're considering an outdoor setting, be sure to add in the weather factor. You may have to move if it begins to rain. And if you miss the rainstorm, you'll still have mud to contend with.

∿ Some economical settings to rent for your ceremony: restaurant, service-club hall, gallery, social or country club, community center, museum, or aquarium.

While some licensed wedding sites charge you a fee up-front to use their property, other equally breathtaking locations are free for the asking. Here are a few places to look.

∿ Have your wedding at a mansion. Check with your local historical society for details, and you'll find a variety of gorgeous homes with some historical significance open to you as a setting for your day. Either hold the festivities indoors, perhaps in the grand dining room, or make use of the mansion's garden and gazebo.

∿ Check with your local historical society for other ideas for free wedding locations. They may be able to direct you to a wonderful and noteworthy spot you'll love.

◇ Consider a winery for an intimate gathering. Many brides find this to be a location more suited to their personality—and pocketbook—than a full-blown extravaganza fit for royalty.

◇ Consider your college or military chapel or banquet hall. As an alumnus or a veteran, you may have access for a limited charge. For instance, the U.S. Naval Academy in Annapolis, Maryland, is a favorite wedding location for Annapolis graduates and members of the navy and marines, among others.

◇ A wedding held at home may be enticing as a free location, but remember to add on the cost of decor and the rental of tables and other necessities. Be sure you won't end up paying more than you would for a modest reception hall location.

◇ Perhaps a friend or relative could offer as their wedding gift to you the use of their yacht or nearby vacation home. Those close to you with resources will undoubtedly be honored that you'd even consider their place for your wedding.

RENTALS FOR A HOME WEDDING

The following is one bride's list of items she had to rent for her at-home wedding. In the end, the cost of the rentals actually added up to more money per guest than if she had held her wedding in a standard banquet hall.

- large tent for reception
- bridal arch for ceremony
- twenty tables for guest seating
- two long tables for buffet
- one hundred fifty chairs
- one hundred fifty sets of china
- one hundred fifty sets of crystal and glassware
- one hundred fifty sets of silverware
- serving platters
- punch bowl
- aisle runner
- portable bar
- installation of dance floor
- platform for band
- booster seats for kids
- and more

A bride who held a smaller wedding inside her home still had to rent china, crystal, glassware, silverware, serving platters, and other items. So be sure to consider the full cost of rentals and the reputation of the rental companies.

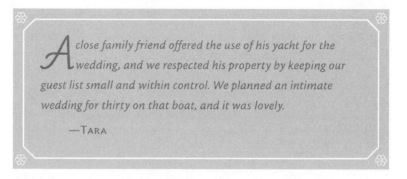

A *close family friend offered the use of his yacht for the wedding, and we respected his property by keeping our guest list small and within control. We planned an intimate wedding for thirty on that boat, and it was lovely.*

—TARA

∽ By all means, never take advantage of a friend who makes an offer to help you out. To do so is the essence of selfishness, and relationships get mangled and ruined through insensitive behavior. Always be sure to respect a friend's home, property, and feelings. Offer to have his or her home professionally cleaned after the wedding and send a thank-you note or gift.

∽ How about a wedding held at a scenic overlook? You'll notice that many fancy reception halls have large picture windows overlooking a glittering city skyline, an inspiring sunset over the water, a blooming valley. To enjoy the same backdrop, you don't have to book a room at three hundred dollars a head; just search for an area with a splendid scenic overlook and make the necessary arrangements with your town to hold your wedding there.

∽ A wedding on the beach is still one of the most romantic choices available to you. For the nominal price of an official license to gather in the oceanside spot you choose and various permissions that are more legwork than check-work, you have available to you a priceless wedding location.

~ Other options include a park, lake, beautiful garden, or arboretum.

~ Try your county's arboretum. For a comfortable fee you'll have access to a banquet hall, a gazebo, and tons of beautiful flowers and floral backdrops for great pictures. Many arboretums feature ponds, brooks, waterfalls, and fountains, all a built-in part of this location that will save thousands on your floral bill.

~ Some locations offer the free services of their own wedding coordinators. These well-studied professionals can save you additional money by advising on what's allowed and not allowed at the site, whether or not the site will already be decorated for the holidays or other special events, and which vendors work at a discount through them.

~ Another inexpensive setting more suitable to the informal or semiformal wedding is a field of flowers. Nothing approaches the beauty of nature more closely than the beauty of matrimony. Again, though, all that beauty may still require a license from your town. Drinking in public and gathering after dark may be against the public order in some regions. A quick check can save you a fortune in tickets.

～ Don't take a standby position on a location schedule just because it's cheaper. There's too much invested in this wedding for you to depend on a maybe for the most important part of the day.

11

The Reception Hall

You don't have to pay top dollar for a wonderful reception location. Here you'll learn how to save when choosing the best reception hall for your wedding.

~ If you've chosen to have your reception at a reception hall, avoid the top-of-the-line places with the largest ads in the newspaper and the celebrity clientele. Their prices will be inflated by their status as a prime wedding location, and they can sometimes be too gaudy for the average person's tastes. Instead, very carefully compare all the choices available to you. Look at the entire package, not just the pretty scenery.

~ Choose a reception location that already has tables, chairs, and equipment so you don't have to rent those separately. Of course, the price for this place may be higher, but you have to consider the value of the items you don't have to rent.

~ When you're checking out reception halls, consider these points: Is the place clean? How many waiters or servers will be working your reception? How many other receptions will there be at the same time as yours? Are the walls soundproof enough to keep out the sounds of the other receptions? Search out all the details that you think could possibly affect your reception, and question the manager about them.

~ Comparison shop among reception locations, and keep track of your notes for each so you can check off what each hall offers for its price. Leave space for notes about each place as well.

~ Consider a smaller, more intimate banquet hall or room for your reception. You may need to trim your guest list slightly, but the price per person is bound to be much lower than for the too-large rooms that drip with crystal and glare with fancy lighting.

~ If your family has a favorite restaurant that you've been going to for years, you obviously already trust its dependability. So don't rule out its reception services just because it's not a new place. That way you don't have to worry whether or not the food will be good. One bride even received a 33 percent–off credit for her wedding at a favorite restaurant's banquet room just because she and her family had been loyal customers for years.

∾ An outdoor setting can add cost for rentals, arrangement of facilities, and more. When you add it all up, make sure you're getting the best deal.

∾ If you're planning an outdoor reception, plan an alternate setting in case it rains. To be doubly sure, map out instructions for a quick move in case the skies break with little time to set up in a new place. Having to hold the wedding on a rain date can mean extra expenses and some lost services with no refunds, so it's smart to have a same-day plan.

∾ The arboretum, winery, mansion, or beach setting you arranged for your ceremony will work just as beautifully for your reception. Besides, having a setting work double duty for you means you won't have to worry about transportation from the ceremony to the reception. That could mean a total of five hundred dollars or more in your pocket. See how savings just pile up when you're looking for them?

∾ One last reception setting option: you can transform a social association's multipurpose party room or a church hall into a pretty locale for your celebration. It may take some extra yards of material, a creative team, and some work, but it can be done nicely. Some organizations even can spruce up the place for you for a small donation to their cause.

The reception location you choose may require you to rent such items as tables, chairs, china, chafing dishes, and linens. Save money in this arena with the following tips.

∼ Know exactly what you need to rent for the reception hall. Get table, floor, and bandstand sizes and have the correct layout and measurements of the room where your wedding will be held. Most reception halls will provide preprinted layouts with dimensions for this use. Always see the items you'll be renting to be sure they're in good condition and to ensure a table for twelve will sit twelve comfortably. Remember that your guests will use more than one plate and glass each. Figure three plates for buffet use, one plate for each course, and several drinking glasses throughout the night. Always order more than you think you'll need, as it would be a major gaffe to run out of clean glasses during your reception. Planning for rental items is a great way to save not just money but the reception's success.

∼ Look at the items you're arranging to rent before you commit to them. The china may be hideous and the glasses chipped.

∼ Carefully review all items when they are delivered, noting broken or marred pieces in order to prevent your having to pay damages. Have the delivery person record the damages and sign this record. Several months ago, a bride didn't get this proof, and the company made her replace twenty chipped wine goblets.

∼ Have the items cleaned afterward, if those are the terms of your contract, and ready to be returned on time. A delay may mean extra charges.

∼ Simply use your own china and glassware if you have enough of a similar style to go around, or borrow from friends and relatives. Items such as punch bowls and candelabras don't need to be rented. You can use your own.

∼ Be sure your rental company is affiliated with the American Rental Association (800-334-2177). You always want to hire a professional.

∼ Be sure delivery is free. If not, ask the groomsmen or family friends to pick up or drop off your rental order.

12

Religious Elements

The officiant comes with a price tag. Booking the church or synagogue may mean extra expenses. Find out how to save on ceremony fees.

~ Comparison shop for officiant fees. Some charge as little as one hundred dollars and some actually ask for six hundred to seven hundred dollars. You can save a lot by knowing that there are some pricing options when shopping for a qualified officiant.

~ Ask your officiant for a copy of the guidelines and restrictions of your church or synagogue. Ask questions to clarify. Certain things may not be allowed in your ceremony—such as a unity candle or a secular song performed by a professional singer—and it's best to find out before you spend money on them.

~ If you need to do some research on the religious elements of your ceremony or reception, skip the seventy-five-dollar religious adviser's fee and talk directly to the wedding officiant.

~ Research customs of your faith in books from the library and articles free on the Internet, or borrow a religious wedding guidebook from a friend or relative.

~ If you need special ceremonial items, such as a satin ring-bearer's pillow, a white aisle runner, a unity candle, or a chuppah, make or borrow them if you can. Or, see if your church or synagogue will allow you to borrow theirs. Mandy regrets not having done this. Her florist charged her one hundred twenty-five dollars for an aisle runner that looked like a giant paper towel roll.

~ Don't plan to add on to any religious ritual or practice unless you've talked to the officiant about it. Most officiants have their own rules, and these must not be crossed or altered without permission. Also, ask if photography and videography are allowed. Some sites forbid intrusive flashes and spotlights.

~ By all means include readings and a performance of music in your religious ceremony. Perhaps reading a religious passage, playing an instrument, or singing a hymn could be a relative's or a friend's gift to you. Make arrangements for *your* soloist to sing or *your* pianist to play, rather than hiring the site's people.

~ If proof of annulment or divorce is needed, don't pay extra fees for the church to locate copies of your legal paperwork. You can send for copies yourself or get free notarized copies of your own documents.

~ Some churches require marrying couples to attend pre-marital classes. If yours is one that does, comparison shop among classes and ask your church if it will accept a certificate of completion from a course taken at another church. Some churches, unfortunately, demand that you take their course at their fee. Take that into consideration when looking for a place to hold your ceremony.

~ If you want a religious officiant to perform your ceremony at a nonreligious site and your church's minister will not comply, look in the Yellow Pages for freelance religious officiants. Research them carefully, checking on their licensing, fees, and other qualifications. Again, prices vary wildly depending on the stature and reputation of the officiant you choose, so put some time into finding the right person to make your marriage binding.

∽ An interesting new development on the officiant scene is that some states ordain people for the day through an uncomplicated application system and a short waiting period. Ordination certificates are also available through the Internet for any interested individuals. If you'd love a family member to perform the service, perhaps he or she can become ordained for the day. Check this carefully, as you need to be sure the credentials are valid.

13

Your Gown

The average bride spends between one thousand and three thousand dollars on her gown. I've even heard of some blank-check brides throwing down a whopping one-hundred-thousand dollars for a dress that's to be worn only once. The wedding gown industry is filled with over-the-top designs and prices to match, but there are plenty of low-cost options that will make you look just as beautiful on your wedding day. Don't think those outrageous price tags are all that's out there. There are ways to get a beautiful gown for less.

～ Start looking right away. Give yourself plenty of time to search out the perfect gown. Most brides who rushed spent hundreds of dollars more on their gowns.

∾ Don't order the gown before you have a date set for the wedding. If you order a summer gown and it turns out your wedding will have to be held in the winter, you'll lose money when you have to cancel your gown and reorder another.

∾ Never order a dress you haven't seen. You could get stuck with something that doesn't match a sketch or description. And you might not get your money back. (Some catalog gowns do have clear return policies.)

∾ Avoid the big, fancy salons. You may think they're a great source of everything you need, and to some brides they may be, but you're also unlikely to get the best prices there. Salons are expensive (how else do you think they pay for all those lights, the plush pink carpeting, and the free cappuccino?), and an aggressive salesperson may pressure you into spending more money than you'd planned. After all, if she works on commission, she gets a bigger cut of whatever you wind up paying. On top of the gown, you may also pay high prices for alterations. So just to be safe and to give yourself a better chance to save money, skip the neon bridal salons.

∾ Call to find out about prices and ordering information. You may even learn that the particular gown you like is being discontinued and therefore offered at a special discount price. One bride found her dream gown this way. She learned it was on the discontinued list, ordered one of the remaining ones in the company's stock, and saved two hundred dollars.

∼ Some gown ads also list the stores and chains where you can find the gown you like. Use the company's list of stores (if you can get to the cities they mention) for your dress hunting so you're confident that you're not buying a copy of a designed gown.

∼ Look through bridal magazines and catalogs to get an idea of what you really like. If you've purchased the magazine or received it as a gift, tear out the pages of the gowns you like and keep them together as possibilities. If you've borrowed the magazine from the library, just mark the pages with a paper clip and bring it along to the stores. Just remember: the gowns pictured on those pages or on websites are not exactly the designer's least expensive options. So don't fall in love with a picture. Be open to finding a less expensive gown of that same style.

BRIDAL GOWN DESIGNERS

To save you some time and keep you organized (and because it is so difficult to keep all of those torn-out pages from magazines in an orderly collection), here are the 800-numbers and websites of some of the biggest gown designers. The ads you'll see in magazines will have the numbers and websites listed, but this list is for quick lookups. Plus, stars indicate the designers who offer the best selection of beautiful gowns and dresses for less than the standard one thousand to three thousand dollars that most brides pay.

Also, be sure to call the designers for your information. Websites provide a look at gowns, but you're best served by talking to an actual sales representative.

*Indicates companies with lower-priced gown options.

Alfred Angelo—800-531-1125

*America's Bridal Discounters—800-326-0833, www.bridaldiscounters.com

*Amsale—212-971-0170, www.amsale.com

Christos, Inc.—212-921-0025, www.christos.com

Emme Bridal—281-634-9225

Forever Yours—800-USA-BRIDE

Galina—212-564-1020

Impressions—800-BRIDAL-1

*Jasmine Collection—630-295-5880

*Jessica McClintock—800-333-5301

Jim Hjelm—800-686-7880

L'Amour—800-664-5683

*Lili—626-336-5048

*Melissa Sweet Bridal Collection—404-633-4395,
    www.melissasweet.com

Michelle Roth—212-245-3390, www.michelleroth.com

Mon Cheri—212-869-0800

Mori Lee—818-385-0930

Pallas Athena—818-285-5796

Priscilla of Boston—617-242-2677, www.priscillaofboston.com

Private Label by G—800-858-3338

Signature Designs—800-654-7375

Silvia Designs—760-323-8808

*Sweetheart—212-947-7171

Tomasina—412-563-7788

*USA Bridal—www.usabridal.com

*Venus—818-285-5796

So where should you look if not in the big bridal salons? Start in smaller bridal salons. You'll find them in the Yellow Pages or in ads in your local newspaper. They need to make less profit on each gown because they don't have to worry about upkeep on their marble floors and chandeliers. Of course, by opting away from the big salon you're sacrificing the posh, first-class service, but if you're determined to save money on nonessentials you'll find the smaller stores offer just as much of what you really need.

I had one gown in mind—and I didn't want any gown but that one. I checked in the big stores and in the catalogs, but no go. I guess it was too simple and classic a style for them to keep in stock. And then one day on a whim I walked into a quaint little bridal store that was no bigger than my kitchen, and there it was! The one gown I wanted, just hanging there like it was waiting for me. The woman behind the counter was so nice, she even suggested an outstanding seamstress whose prices were the lowest in the area. I was so pleased, I ordered my bridesmaids' gowns from there too.

—SHEA

≈ If you're able to, look at bridal stores in different parts of your city, different cities, even different states. In a "richer" area, you're likely to find that prices are higher because the clientele can afford the amount asked. In more middle-class areas, prices are a bit lower. You may be able to find your dream dress across town for a hundred dollars less. Or your cousin in

Delaware may find the dress for much less than its New York price tag.

❧ When you're searching for a gown in several bridal shops, comparison shop like crazy. Take note of each store's policy on alterations, ordering time, refund rules, and flexibility. Check the quality of their work. Is the on-site seamstress frazzled and looking way behind schedule? Is the stock in good condition and relatively new? What kinds of guarantees can they give you? It pays to put in the time to compare the places that might outfit you on your wedding day. You'll want the best quality service your budget can buy. One bride used a notebook to record facts, figures, and observations about each bridal shop she considered. Her research paid off well—the shop she chose ended up saving her two hundred dollars more than the others would have.

❧ If you have a friend or relative who works in a dress shop or a department store, see if she'll let you use her employee's discount. Ten to 20 percent off a five-hundred-dollar gown is a savings of fifty to a hundred dollars.

❧ Look in bridal sections of major department stores. While business there may have been crowded out in the past by fancy salons, brides today are coming back to the basics in gown shopping. They're looking for quality and a good price again, so the glitz of a salon may not be their first choice anymore.

∽ When narrowing down choices, check with your state's Better Business Bureau to see if the companies are clear. Have there been any complaints or reports against them? At worst, are they operating illegally? We've all heard the horror stories about the dress shops that mysteriously disappeared in the middle of the night, leaving hundreds of brides without their gowns and the thousands of dollars they paid for them the week before the wedding. Unfortunately, it has happened and it could happen again. So consult the reporting agency to see if your store is legitimate and free of suspicious record. When you're dealing with something as important as your gown, it's best to protect yourself from all angles.

∽ Be sure the gown you choose fits the level of formality of your wedding. You won't wear an ultraformal gown with a ten-foot train to a tea party in the garden. Staying within your level of formality will keep you from spending too much on a too-fancy gown.

∽ Make sure the gown is of good quality. Inspect the seams and stitches to ensure that it's been made well. You don't want your investment to fall apart on you.

∼ Buy a simple gown. Beads and bangles raise the price of the gown and the care it requires. If you like the beaded look, you can always add your own or have a friend do the work for you. Tammy bought a simple gown for two hundred dollars and bought fifty dollars worth of pearls and beads to stitch onto her neckline and bodice. When she was finished, her wedding gown looked identical to an eight-hundred-dollar store-bought wedding gown.

∼ Buy a gown in a less expensive material. Do your homework on fabric prices. Compare satin, taffeta, silk, crisp cotton, and so on.

∼ A shorter, tea-length or suit dress is of course going to be less expensive than a full-length gown with a ten-foot train. Just make sure it fits the formality of your wedding.

∼ Shop the sales, particularly after-holiday sales. Included in this discount category is the sale rack on which you'll find discontinued gowns, sample gowns marked down, and last season's still-fabulous styles the store is trying to move out of its inventory.

∼ Check out nonbridal gowns such as the many beautifully designed, elegant, white or off-white prom gowns that are on the market today, holiday formal gowns, even bridesmaid's gowns. Being nonbridal, and not requiring ordering and delivery, these gowns can be found at much lower prices.

∾ Don't miss designer trunk shows and sample sales where designer gowns can be found at markdowns as low as 60 to 70 percent off. You'll find advertisements for these wonderful sales in bridal magazines, on bridal websites, and in the newspaper's special bridal inserts. Some bridal salons even host trunk shows of their own, so call and ask for schedules and appointments.

∾ Some bridal shops have sample sales of their own stocked gowns. Just remember that although the savings may be great, many women before you have tried on these gowns, which may have smudges and stains. Shop wisely and you may find a wonderful discount on a gown you can take home that day.

∾ Did you ever think while you were walking through a regular dress shop, "I wish this pretty white dress was a wedding dress. It would be perfect for me."? Well, get it and turn it into a wedding dress. Just because the pretty white dress is on the prom gown rack, the bridesmaid's rack, or even the New Year's special rack doesn't mean it won't do. No one said the label has to read "Certified Wedding Gown" for you to wear it to your wedding. In fact, since everything labeled with the words *wedding* or *bridal* is by nature elevated in price, you're saving money just by looking in the nonbridal dress section. And wouldn't it be wonderful to buy your wedding gown for under a hundred dollars?

∽ If you find that a full-priced gown on a dress shop rack has a tiny, fixable flaw, ask the store manager if you can have that gown for a discount. After all, other brides might not take it in its current condition. A flawed gown can almost always be mended. So don't walk past that "irregular" rack, either.

∽ Maya found a pretty off-white gown that had a torn side seam. A simple repair would do the trick, *she* knew, but the store considered it damaged goods and knocked seventy-five dollars off the price just to get it off their rack.

∽ Ask the manager when the new shipment of gowns is scheduled to arrive. With advance notice, you might be able to beat the crowds for the nicest but most inexpensive in the bunch.

∽ Don't trust a sale sign without checking to see if the price is really better. The thousand-dollar price tag you see marked out in red pen, then replaced with a seven-hundred-fifty-dollar tag may just be a ploy to make you think you're getting a huge discount. This is where comparison shopping is crucial.

～ When shopping, the input of others can influence you to choose a more expensive gown. If everyone is cooing "Oh, you look *fabulous* in that other one," you may be swayed by group opinion to choose a more expensive gown than the one you love equally. The best shopping strategy is to go by yourself or with one other person for an objective opinion.

～ Shop early in the day. You have more energy for comparison shopping, and you're more likely to be focused on the one job at hand.

～ Brides-to-be have found beautiful gowns for as little as forty or fifty dollars at the outlets. Look in your Yellow Pages or on the Internet for outlet stores, and head out for a day of sure-thing cut prices up to 60 percent, 70 percent, even 80 percent off. To find outlets near you, or to learn more about the benefits of outlet shopping, write, call, or check your library or bookstore for this publication:

> *The Joy of Outlet Shopping*, The Outlet Consumer
> Reporter, P.O. Box 7867, St. Petersburg, FL 33734,
> Outlet Bound 800-336-8853

～ Believe it or not, some of the most beautiful ivory and off-white gowns can be found at antique shops. Krissy found a 1930 antique hand-beaded wedding dress for under two hundred dollars. Scout the shops in the center of town, ask for help (most antique-store owners are aware of what's in stock in other antique stores), and even browse through some of the antique shows you've seen advertised in the paper.

~ Research cast-off gowns in consignment shops and classified ads. You wouldn't believe the quality and beauty of some of the gowns I've seen in consignment shops. When I asked about their origins, I heard many understandable stories. Some brides who canceled their weddings couldn't return their gowns and now would settle for one hundred dollars for a one-thousand-dollar gown. Some brides ordered gowns over the Internet that didn't fit and now have to unload the nonreturnable item for a fraction of what they paid. Some divorcing women just want their well-preserved wedding gowns out of the house. Brides who gave up on family squabbling and eloped may now have a formal gown to sell. Whatever the story, the result is the same: these are beautiful gowns that you can have for far less than retail prices.

~ When choosing your gown, no matter where you're shopping, always consider your body type and whether that dress is right for you. Does it make you look shorter? Is it accentuating your hips? Is it too tight? Is it too low cut? You don't want to buy a dress that doesn't make you look your best.

〜 Order your correct dress size according to the manufacturer's measurements so you won't have to pay for major alterations. Some dress shops order larger sizes intentionally so the buyer has to pay to have the dress taken in. Similarly, don't order a dress size smaller than what you are right now because you're planning to lose thirty pounds by your wedding day. At worst, you won't lose all the weight and you'll be stuck with a too-small gown that doesn't look good on you. Instead, order your current size and don't worry about the cost of alterations.

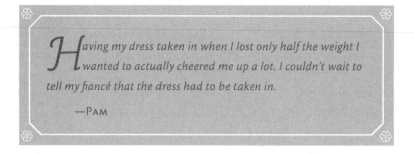

Having my dress taken in when I lost only half the weight I wanted to actually cheered me up a lot. I couldn't wait to tell my fiancé that the dress had to be taken in.

—PAM

〜 Order a wedding gown that can be cut to a shorter length, trimmed of embellishments, and worn again. It's good money sense to spend that much for a dress you *will* be able to wear again.

〜 Don't leave deposits on several gowns in different stores when you're just looking. You may not get that money back, and there's really no need to believe the saleswoman who's trying to get you to believe a busload of brides might just order every last one in the next day or two. Leave a deposit only when you're sure.

～ When paying for your gown, use a credit card. You'll have an easier time getting reimbursed if something should go wrong.

～ Keep all sales slips as a record of the date you ordered the dress, the specifics of the dress, and its size, and as added precaution, get the salesperson to sign it as a record of who sold the dress to you. Trouble can be cleared up easily with that information. In addition, have the seamstress write down your measurements and the store-recommended dress size on the order form. If a gown is ordered that's too small and a reorder is necessary, you'll have the proof for them to pay expenses.

～ Keep a record of the promised date of delivery, too, so you can get on the phone if your dress is late.

～ Rent your gown. This option is becoming wildly popular, especially as designer gown prices are soaring to five figures. Qualified rental agencies stock beautiful designer gowns and most shops have a policy that they will only rent each gown three or four times. You can wear a drop-dead gorgeous designer gown on your wedding day for three hundred dollars rather than own a cheap frock for the same amount of money.

⮑ Seamstresses or dressmakers can be hired to make the gown for you from scratch. You provide the material and pattern, of course, and then pay her for the work. This custom method of creating your dress may not bring as much savings as some of the other ideas, but it's a definite chop off the store-bought prices you'll find.

⮑ Some seamstresses do a little bit of moonlighting. Several travel to big cities on buyer's trips, frequenting discount shops, showrooms, designers, and secondhand boutiques in trendier areas in search of simple and inexpensive wedding dresses to mend and embellish to sell for profit. Call around to see if any nearby seamstresses perform that service, and then arrange to take a look. You may even find the occasional designer original with a price you can manage. The seamstress who worked on my wedding gown took me to her projects room and showed me her collection of thirty wedding gowns she found for less than wholesale at the showroom sale: all were to be fixed up and sold for half their full retail price. I called all my friends and alerted them to this gold mine.

～ During fittings, ensure the correct fit by wearing the bra, slip, and shoes you'll be wearing on your wedding day. They can affect the way the dress hangs on you and wearing them at every fitting will save you money on last-minute alterations. And *always* get receipts for your fittings.

One bride unfortunately had to pay fifty dollars in last-minute alteration fees at her final fitting because her selection of wedding underwear made the dress a little too snug. Yet another bride found that her new corset-style strapless bra was just enough to keep the back zipper on her gown from closing all the way, so she had to do without it.

14

Your Shoes and Accessories

Two hundred dollars for a pair of simple, white shoes?! I'm amazed at what some brides will spend to have the best of everything on their wedding day. Your shoes and accessories are just a small part of your wedding look, accents to your radiant beauty. Read on to learn how to get great shoes and accessories without spending a fortune.

*Y*our Shoes

⁓ Don't order shoes in a bridal salon. The price will be much higher than in a regular shoe store. One price test turned up a fifty-dollar difference in identical shoes sold at a regular store versus a bridal salon.

～ For a great price cut, order the same style shoes your bridesmaids will be wearing so you're a part of their group order discount. Yours may even be free with a group order of, say, four pairs or more. Just be sure your pair isn't sent to be dyed with theirs.

～ The top priority in the choice of your shoes, since they'll most likely be hidden for most of the day, is comfort. Choose a style and heel height that won't make you feel all blistered and sore.

～ Choose plain shoes over fancy, decorated ones. Each bead and sewn-in design costs money.

COMPARE AND SAVE
Beaded, appliquéd shoes $125
Plain ½" heel shoes $40

～ Look in the Yellow Pages for a discount shoe store and shop there. Inspect your choices for quality as well as price. A fifteen-dollar pair of shoes is no bargain if they fall apart after two uses.

﹏ Look for seasonal shoe sales. A 50 percent clearance will take the bite out of shoe prices.

﹏ Wear ballerina slippers. They're light and comfortable, they look charming and romantic, and they're inexpensive as well. At the right store or in a dancer's supply catalog, like Capezio, you can find these for as low as ten dollars a pair. Look in the Yellow Pages under Dancing Supplies.

﹏ Check out a few antique stores for those pretty antique lace-up boots. You might just beat the prices offered in bridal salons and lingerie catalogs.

﹏ Shop for your shoes later in the afternoon when your feet are naturally swollen. Shoes that fit in the morning may be tight on you during your evening reception, so think ahead and use a general rule of shoe shopping.

﹏ While trying on shoes, be sure you're wearing stockings rather than socks. Either wear your own, or if you're caught without and have just found a great sale, use the footsie stockings available to shoe-store patrons for this very purpose. It's a good idea to carry your own pair of knee-highs or footsie stockings in your purse when you're shoe shopping.

↝ For the ultimate in savings, wear a pair of white dress shoes you already own. Just make sure they look nice, not old, scraped, and worn in the heel. You may be lifting up your dress to reveal your garter later on in the reception, and you won't want to reveal your savings in the shoe department at the same time. Warning: this only works if your already owned shoes are suitable for the formality of your wedding. Many brides have used this idea and have reported that they loved being in comfortable, broken-in shoes they knew would fit.

↝ Scuff up the bottoms of your shoes for traction, and wear your shoes around the house for a few days before the wedding to break them in. You don't want stiff, slippery shoes on your wedding day. Better to be safe and comfortable than not.

Your Veil

The veil you'll wear depends on the formality of your wedding and your dress. Be sure of the basics before you shop, to avoid having to return your choice for a loss of money.

↝ Comparison shop for veils in bridal salons' sale racks. You won't have to sacrifice frugality for selection. Or look through bridal and discount catalogs for a reasonably priced veil.

~ Veils can be rented, if you're not superstitious about previously worn wedding attire.

~ Wear your mother's wedding veil. It will mean a lot to both of you, and you'll probably only have to pay for a cleaning and alteration to your height. Or borrow a relative's veil if she seems receptive to the idea. Siblings, grandmothers, godmothers, great-grandparents—all are likely to bestow the honor.

~ Have a talented relative or friend make your veil for you, using a fabric headband, some pearls, and netting. Tear out a picture of the kind of veil you'd like, and accept the artist's work as her gift to you. Or make your own veil if you have the time and the talent. One bride's aunt made the bride's veil from some tulle, a fabric headband, and some pearls. Her gorgeous creation cost just thirty dollars to make and was even prettier than the two-hundred-dollar styles in the stores.

~ You can find easy-to-use make-your-own-veil kits at most major craft stores. These come with standard hair combs and headbands, material, and accessories, plus simple instructions for a talented crafter to use. Compared to bridal shop prices of three hundred to five hundred dollars for a veil, this twenty-five-dollar investment saves a bundle.

~ For informal or nonreligious weddings, it may be appropriate for you to go without a veil. Check your etiquette books, search your options, and decide.

Your Headcovering

~ An arrangement of baby rosebuds and baby's breath can be tucked into a hair clip that holds up a French twist. There's no need to order this to be made at extra cost by your florist; just experiment ahead of time and do it yourself.

~ For a beautiful, original look, try pearl hairpins or any number of styles of hair decor and tiaras that you'll find in the accessories store in your mall. Avoid the department store counters—they'll try to entice you with their counters full of real pearl headpieces. Those inexpensive accessory places offer some nice, simple styles (among the more trendy, teenybopper choices), so search well. Some brides report that they found beautiful, simple pearl hair-decor pins for ten dollars. Sparkling "diamond-style" pins went for twelve to fifteen dollars. Compare that to the four-hundred-dollar simple pearl headpiece I found in a department store.

◇ Or choose instead not to wear any headcovering at all. Just make sure this option conforms to your wedding location's rules and the degree of formality of the wedding.

◇ Skip the veil and headpiece and just let your hair be the focal point of your look. Talented hairstylists can create veritable sculptures from your hair using upsweeps, twists, braids, and tendrils. Accentuate your 'do with inexpensive pearl or jeweled hairpins or tiny fresh flowers, and you've only spent thirty to forty dollars.

Your Slip

◇ Don't buy your slip in a bridal salon if you can help it. By now you must have realized that bridal salons are far more expensive than other options. Check in department store bridal and undergarment departments for slips and skirts that will do just as nicely . . . for one-half to one-third of what you would have spent in the bridal salon.

◇ Don't pay extra for a bridal slip or crinoline at the bridal salon. Many gowns now have crinolines built in them for no extra charge.

～ Do you really need a slip? Check your dress out in all lighting—indoors, outdoors, direct sunlight, spotlights—to see if you can get away with wearing one less layer.

Your Garter

～ Since you'll undoubtedly want to keep your garter as a precious memento of your wedding day, you should have two garters: one to keep and one to throw. Buy what brides call a "cheapie" in a lingerie store for the tossing. Note: the garter toss is becoming passé. You may choose to skip this outdated custom entirely.

Your Stockings and Lingerie

～ Buy basic stockings. While the fancy silk kinds with patterns or the little design at the ankle are great indulgences for the bride, they're also a place where money can be saved without noticeable loss. You'll feel just as wonderful on your wedding day whether or not your stockings cost forty dollars. (Try L'Eggs or Hanes for the best in quality at a reasonable price. Skip the designer labels and the bridal design stockings in white with heart or dove accents at the ankles or seams.)

~ Sexy, silky lingerie under your gown can make you even more radiant on your wedding day, but you can save money on your bra, teddy, panties, or G-string. Rather than buy a new set for your wedding day, wear the lacy white number you already have, or use the Victoria's Secret gift certificate you received at your shower.

~ Shop for your wedding bra and panties in catalogs or in discount stores, or watch for clearance sales at Victoria's Secret. They offer two-for-one sales, half-off prices, and free gifts with purchases. Visit them at www.victoriassecret.com. (Hint: their catalog sales are better than their featured on-line quotes, so get a catalog.)

~ If you have either a small chest or a fairly structured gown, don't wear a bra under your gown. How's that for savings?

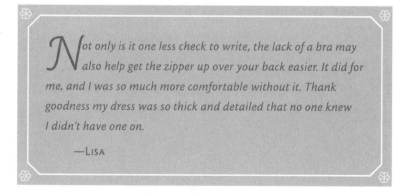

Not only is it one less check to write, the lack of a bra may also help get the zipper up over your back easier. It did for me, and I was so much more comfortable without it. Thank goodness my dress was so thick and detailed that no one knew I didn't have one on.

—LISA

∼ Have an extra pair of stockings in your emergency bag (more on this later) in case of a noticeable run. If you have splurged on expensive silk stockings for your originals, the extra pair definitely should be the more generic of the two you've purchased.

∼ Skip all the extras, like gloves and parasols. They're the essence of nonessential. One bride's total for gloves, a parasol, and jeweled hair clips for under her veil was one hundred eighty dollars. That amount could be better used elsewhere. Like the honeymoon.

Your Jewelry

∼ Don't buy new jewelry for your wedding. It's very likely that your groom's wedding gift to you will be fine jewelry of some sort, and you'll want to wear that.

> *I didn't know Michael had already bought me a pearl necklace to wear on our wedding day, and unfortunately I went out and bought myself one, on sale, too. It couldn't be returned.*
>
> —CARRIE

∼ Jewelry, if not a gift, also makes a wonderful "something borrowed" choice. Wear an heirloom necklace or earrings, perhaps the pearls your mother wore at her wedding.

Cash Bag

∼ Rather than buy an expensive beaded bag in which to keep the cards and checks given to you by guests at your wedding, make a simple satin bag yourself or . . . borrow a relative's or friend's decorative cash bag. Older, discolored ones can be cleaned carefully.

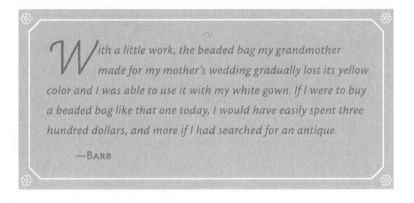

With a little work, the beaded bag my grandmother made for my mother's wedding gradually lost its yellow color and I was able to use it with my white gown. If I were to buy a beaded bag like that one today, I would have easily spent three hundred dollars, and more if I had searched for an antique.

—BARB

15

Dressing the Bridal Party

Your attendants are honored to be chosen as part of your bridal party, but you don't want to sour the mood by burdening them with too high a financial commitment for their wedding day attire. Here you'll find out how to make the right selections to save them money.

Bridesmaids and Junior Bridesmaids

Bridesmaids' Gowns

~ While some brides like to purchase their bridesmaids' gowns as gifts for them, you'd do well to allow them to buy their own dresses. Most expect that they'll have to anyway.

BRIDESMAIDS' AND MOTHER OF THE BRIDE'S GOWNS

Indicates companies with lower-priced gown options.

Alfred Angelo—800-531-1125

Bianchi—800-669-2346

*Bill Levkoff—800-LEVKOFF

Chadwick's of Boston Special Occasions—800-525-6650

Champagne Formals—212-302-9162

Dessy Creations—800-633-7791

Entourage—212-719-0889

Galina—212-564-1020

*JCPenney—800-527-8347, www.jcpenney.com

*Jessica McClintock—800-333-5301

*Macy's—877-622-9274, www.macys.weddingchannel.com

*Melissa Sweet Bridal Collection—404-633-4395,
   www.melissasweet.com

Spiegel—800-527-1577, www.spiegel.com

Watters and Watters—972-960-9884, www.watters.com

∼ Look at the bridesmaids' gowns shown in bridal magazines to get a feel for the current styles and colors, and call the printed toll-free numbers of the stores listed in the advertisements for the price range. Your research will be a great help when it's time to go dress hunting.

✑ Just as you were encouraged to order your gown directly from the manufacturer listed in the advertisement in a bridal magazine, you can do the same for your maids' gowns to be sure you're not getting a copy at original prices.

✑ Go with your maids to the dress shop so that you'll all have a say in the dresses they'll be wearing. You'll want them to choose a dress to match the formality of your wedding and to complement your gown, and they'll want to make sure a completely unflattering style and color are not chosen for them. One bride, for instance, chose a dress for all four of her attendants. The two women with larger-than-average chests looked even larger, and the other two looked like sticks. No one was happy, especially at one hundred thirty dollars a dress.

✑ Let the maids choose their own styles of gowns in their price ranges in the same color, ideally from the same store. Everyone will coordinate well and you eliminate the hassles of who can't afford the gown that the other maids love and whose derriere is too big for that style. Everyone gets a gown that fits them well, compliments their shape, fits their budget, and suits the formality of the occasion.

✑ If you have only two or three bridesmaids, you should look for dresses in department stores. A store is more likely to have enough gowns on the rack in your maids' sizes. That wouldn't be the case with eight maids, more than likely, so you've saved again by choosing a smaller bridal party.

～ Always hunt for group discounts when you're looking for bridesmaids' dresses. Ask even if one isn't offered. Marisa made the question of group discounts a part of her search and comparisons of stores. When she found a company that offered group discounts, each of her attendants saved 20 percent on her dress.

～ Another reason to look in department stores for your maids' gowns is that prices there are likely to be much lower than those in the bridal shops. Also look in smaller dress shops for better prices and perhaps better service.

～ Prom and party dresses are very often ordered as bridesmaids' gowns. Just be sure to shop outside of prom season because prices may be elevated due to demand. The best time to shop may be pre–pre-prom season and post-prom season when dressy dresses are overstocked and up for clearance. Pretty bridesmaids' dresses can be found on the post-prom rack for as low as thirty dollars, marked down from one hundred twenty dollars.

~ Shop at outlets, perhaps when you're hunting through the Gunne Sax outlet for your own gown. Again, researchers found dresses at 50 to 60 percent off.

~ Attend sample sales and trunk shows to get your maids 60 to 70 percent off their designer gowns.

~ If you have only one or two bridesmaids, you might find complementary gowns in an antique shop for a fraction of what salons charge for the "heirloom look."

~ Wherever you're shopping, encourage the maids to choose a gown style according to their budget, not yours. You'll all feel better.

~ Encourage your maids to choose a style of dress they'll be able to wear again to formal dinners, dances, and the like. A hundred-dollar dress is a better deal when it's used ten times.

~ Keep in mind that simpler dresses are often less expensive than detailed, sexy ones. Aside from the price, the maids shouldn't look provocative on your wedding day.

∼ Consider having your maids rent their dresses. Ultraformal gowns can be found for the price of casuals. No one has to know the dresses are rented.

∼ Shop at bridal shops that offer free alterations. If the bridal shop charges for its alteration package, you might choose to pass. Hint: do *not* depend on a friend for this. Go professional; a shoddy sewing job is a big glaring example of trying too hard to save.

∼ Find a good seamstress or tailor to hire for much less than the dress shop's rates. Get references and comparison shop. Savings here can be anywhere from fifty to a hundred dollars.

∼ If your bridesmaids all live in different cities, have them send you their professionally taken measurements on size cards and checks for their dresses. Then you take those size cards to the dress shop you've chosen so that you can order your maids' gowns for them.

∼ Do not allow your maids to order their gowns in shops near their homes because batches of gowns may differ in hue according to which factory they were made in. Always order the gowns in one place, then send them to your maids.

⌒ Send the gowns via priority mail, and insure them when you mail them to your maids. This is no time for a dress to get lost in the mail. If you're nervous about this, ask your bridesmaids to let you know when their packages arrive. Or attach return postcards on each package so you'll be notified of safe delivery. Federal Express or UPS may be an extra expense, but it's well worth it because missing shipments can be tracked.

⌒ As an alternative to this setup, assign your maid or matron of honor the task of ordering and delivering gowns, especially if she lives close to the bridesmaids while you're farther away. One bride saved over fifty dollars in shipping and communications this way.

Shoes

⌒ Comparison shop at different shoe stores and research the prices of those styles you see in the magazines.

⌒ Shoes, for the same reason as gowns, must be ordered in the same place. Differences in shoe colors among your maids can ruin your bridal party's look, so arrange to order as a group. The best way to do this is to pick out a shoe style at a national chain of shoe stores, get the style number from the clerk, then ask your maids to go and try on that particular shoe in the same chain's stores near them. You know that a size seven in one style may be the same as a nine in another, so it's best to help your maids order shoes that will fit them correctly. Once the maids have their sizes in the style you've chosen, you can more accurately order their shoes for them.

SHOES AND ACCESSORIES

Indicates companies with lower-priced merchandise options. Check your local sources for on-sale accessories.

Shoes and Handbags

Capezio—212-245-2130

Kenneth Cole—800-KENCOLE

*Dyeables—800-431-2000

Fenaroli for Regalia—617-723-3682

Neiman Marcus—310-550-5900

Watters and Watters—972-960-9884, www.watters.com

Also check your local Marty's Shoes or discount shoe stores for quality choices.

Veils and Headpieces

Dream Veils and Accessories—312-943-9554,
    www.dreamveilsacc.com

Fenaroli for Regalia—617-723-3682

Homa—973-467-5500, homabridal@aol.com

Jessica McClintock—800-333-5301

Renee Romano—312-943-0912, www.Renee-Romano.com

Tia Mazza—212-989-4349

~ Try for a group discount when you're ordering shoes. Talk to the store manager if you have to. It's possible that your pair of shoes could be given to you free of charge if your order is large enough.

~ Rather than mailing the shoes to your maids, consider holding onto them at your house so they won't have to travel with bulky shoe boxes to your place for the wedding. Give the shoes to your maids a few days before the wedding so they can break them in and scuff the soles a bit to prevent slipping.

Headpieces

~ Decorate the maids' French-braided or upswept hairstyles with wisps of baby's breath or pearl pins from an accessory shop. The price: ten to fifteen dollars.

~ It's perfectly fine for your maids not to adorn their hair at all. In fact, it's quite classy. Let the ringlets or French twist be design enough.

Slips and Stockings

~ Allow each maid to wear her own slip (of an appropriate length and color) under her gown. There's no need for your attendants to buy new undergarments for your wedding.

For a uniform look, though, your maids should wear the same brand and color stockings. Either take their order and pick up two pairs for each maid, or have your maid or matron of honor do this for you. A good way to save money on stockings (up to 50 percent) is to choose plain pairs over the fancy, silky, name-brand styles. (Keep the stockings at your house so everyone has the right stockings waiting for her when she arrives on the morning of the wedding.)

Accessories

Inexpensive gloves may be found at department stores if you want them. Those you see at bridal salons are probably overpriced, so check elsewhere first.

If your wedding isn't a formal one, you may choose not to have your maids wear gloves.

Flower Girls

Dresses

Their mothers usually buy the flower girls' dresses, so do them a favor by suggesting an inexpensive style the little girls can use again.

⁓ Your flower girls can get a second wearing out of their First Communion or party dresses. Either leave the dresses unadorned or incorporate your color scheme through the use of ribbons, lace, a sash, or trim. For the price of just a fabric sash (eight dollars), flower girl Lauren's fancy white party dress became her dress for the wedding. She saved her family fifty-five dollars by not needing a new dress for that day.

⁓ Check out children's discount stores for your flower girls. You'll find a great variety of children's party dresses and more formal dresses, plus a wide selection of wedding-ready whites and pastels at post-Easter sales. Remember that plain white or off-white children's dresses can be dressed up to match your bridal party's colors with the easy addition of a sash at the waist.

⁓ Have your flower girls' dresses made, either by a talented relative, a friend, or an inexpensive seamstress. And shop at fabric sales for the material for the flower girls' dresses. You won't need much. A smart shopper can assemble supplies for each flower-girl dress for thirty to forty dollars per dress.

Shoes

⁓ Flower girls may wear their own party shoes or their dancing school ballet slippers.

~ Get kids' party shoes at discount shoe stores or national discount chains such as Kohl's, Target, or Kmart. There's absolutely no need to get the flower girls' shoes at a bridal salon, no matter how pretty the styles.

Headpieces

~ Wreaths of flowers look charming on the heads of flower girls, so consider this simple look for your wedding.

Accessories

~ Borrow a basket from a friend for each flower girl to carry during the ceremony. One bride saved the baskets that once held floral bouquets her fiancé had sent—double use and a good savings on extras.

The Groom, the Groomsmen, and the Fathers of the Bride and Groom

As the men most likely will be wearing identical tuxedos or similar suits, they're grouped together here. This condensed listing does not, of course, reflect any diminished importance of the men involved in the wedding process.

The Tuxedo or Suit

〜 Again, look at plenty of pictures in magazines and brochures to get an idea of the colors, fabrics, styles, and prices that suit your group best. Look at a picture of the tuxedo next to a picture of the bridesmaids' gowns. Make sure they look good together.

〜 Ask recently married friends to recommend the tuxedo rental shop they used for their wedding. This way, you'll have an idea of the business's reliability and quality.

〜 Always compare prices at tuxedo rental agencies around town. Companies to look for in your phone book are those that offer Gingiss Formalwear, Lord West, Henry Grethel, and so on.

〜 Look for a reputable tuxedo rental agency that offers group discounts.

〜 Ask if the groom gets his tuxedo free with your groomsmen's order or if the free tux can go to your father.

⁓ If the groomsmen and the fathers of the bride and groom are many miles away at the time of the tuxedo order, have the men send in their measurements on size cards so the correct tuxedos can be ordered for them. Be sure they get their measurements taken at a professional tailor's shop—again, no ruler and string job—so that the numbers are reliable.

⁓ Schedule tailoring for several days before the wedding . . . in case of a problem. If a problem were to be found at the last minute, extra charges would be made for rushed alterations.

⁓ If the men will be wearing dark suits, their minor expense will be identical ties. Look in a discount store or at a department store sale for these. Check Marshall's, Today's Man, or NBO for good values.

⁓ Make sure you get a signed copy of the contract or order receipt to verify your order in case of a mix-up. Record the style number, style name, sizes, deposit amount, check number, delivery date, and the name of the clerk who took your tuxedo order. Good record keeping ensures that any questions or mistakes made by the tuxedo agency can be cleared up quickly. Call several times to confirm the order and availability of the tuxedos—just to make sure.

⁓ If your groomsmen will be wearing dark suits instead of tuxedos, as in the case of an informal wedding, they will undoubtedly be wearing suits they already own. But just to be sure their look will be appropriate, arrange for the men to wear the suits ahead of time for you (perhaps to a dinner party). This way, you can check to see that their versions of dark are really dark, that the suits are in good order and style, and that leg and arm lengths aren't too short. You have a right to preview what the men will be wearing, so if they complain about the scrutiny, just tell them that the plans could be changed if they wish. They could always shell out for a tuxedo. You won't believe how quickly they'll have their suits tailored.

Shoes

⁓ Shoes can be rented at a group discount rate from the tuxedo rental shop.

⁓ The men can wear their own dark shoes if the dark suits will be their wedding day wardrobe. Again, arrange to see the shoes ahead of time.

$\mathcal{R}ing$ Bearers

Suits

~ If the boy will be renting a tuxedo, try to get a discount at the store you've chosen as your men's outfitter.

~ Allow the ring bearer to wear his own suit, with a new bow tie to match the bridal party's color scheme.

~ As many brides know, the young ring bearer will look adorable in white shorts and a white shirt with a little cummerbund and a bow tie. The clothes may be his own, while the tie and cummerbund may be made with ease. This is a popular new practice, as it is both a charming look and a big savings.

Shoes

~ Find a child's discount shoe store and look for an inexpensive style, or the ring bearer may wear a pair of his own dress shoes if they're appropriate.

16

Dressing the Mothers
of the Bride and Groom

*No, you don't have to buy their gowns. You're just being a dutiful
daughter (and daughter-in-law) by helping the mothers choose their
best and most affordable look for your wedding day. Many brides like
having a say in what the mothers wear, as it's lovely to have the moms
in complementary colors and styles in the family wedding portraits.*

The Dress

~ Look through magazines with your mother so both of you
can discuss what kinds of dresses will be appropriate and which
colors you prefer. This way, you won't have to accompany your
mother to every dress shop she wants to "just take a look in,"

and you won't have to fear her choice when she announces she's found the perfect dress.

∿ Remember the mothers' dresses should adhere to the formality of your wedding. That means long gowns are out if the bridesmaids are wearing tea-length dresses. In essence, the mothers of the bride and groom are an extended part of the bridal party, so wardrobe rules apply to them as well. Besides, shorter, less formal gowns usually aren't as expensive as those floor-length, beaded numbers.

∿ The mothers' gowns should be somewhat conservative in order not to outdo the bride's, and you will also avoid the extra expense of a flashier style.

∿ Avoid bridal salons for the mothers' dresses. As you know by now, prices here are often much higher than those of non-specialized dress shops. Look in the formal section of a regular department store. Prices are bound to be lower than in the salon, and you may chance upon a sale. Identical gowns were seen in a bridal salon priced at two hundred fifty dollars and at a regular dress shop for one hundred seventy-five dollars.

∿ Speaking of sales, shop for the mothers' gowns after major holidays. After-event overstock may be reduced in price for clearance.

◡ Consider shopping for the mother of the bride's and the mother of the groom's dresses in an outlet store for a considerable discount. You'll find savings up to 60 percent off or more in some national outlets.

◡ Buy a very simple gown in a department or discount store and add a jeweled neckline or fancy trim.

◡ Check into formal dress rentals for both mothers, a much less expensive alternative to buying.

◡ If the groom's mother lives far away from you or your mother, send her a swatch and a picture of the gown your mother has chosen so she can then make her selection. The mother of the bride chooses her dress first as an honor, and the mother of the groom should wear a similar but not identical style and a similar color. It looks better in the wedding photos if the mothers are in complementary rather than clashing colors.

The Shoes

◡ Avoid shoe selections at the bridal salon. They may be overpriced. Instead, comparison shop among the larger shoe chains in your area.

～ Order the mothers' shoes with yours and your brides-maids' for an even better group discount rate, if available. Remember to ask.

～ Encourage the mothers to buy simpler shoes.

Accessories

～ To save them money, encourage both mothers to wear their own jewelry and to forgo headpieces or hats.

～ Except perhaps in ultraformal weddings, gloves are optional for the mothers of the bride and groom. They may even be inappropriate for a less formal wedding. So decide what would look best, and if gloves are indeed included, either look for good discounts, or allow the mothers of the bride and groom to wear gloves they already own.

17

Keepsakes

It's great to have keepsakes of your big day, but you don't need to invest in some of the marketing gimmicks that are available today. You can create your own or your loved ones' keepsakes at a fraction of catalog costs, and they will have more personalized meaning.

⁓ To record your planning experiences—which are always fun to look back on—keep a journal in a plain, lined notebook. The fancy bridal journals on the market are not one page longer than these and they do the same job, yet they may be double or triple in cost.

COMPARE AND SAVE

Bridal journal .... $30–$40

Plain journal .... $5–$10

∽ Charge up the home video camera and take your own footage throughout the wedding planning months and on the morning of the wedding. It's ridiculous to pay a professional photographer to record your rehearsal and the four hours it takes to get everyone ready before the ceremony. Besides, home movies are far more personal and fun than those taken by a stranger.

∽ Make your own wedding memorabilia scrap box, in which you'll put swatches of material, favors, menus, and all the little meaningful items you wouldn't dare throw away. Bridal stores sell these types of decorated memorabilia boxes, but you can beat their price by covering a large cardboard box with either satiny material or bridal wrapping paper, lace, ribbons, bows, and a print label of the contents.

COMPARE AND SAVE

Store-bought memorabilia box .... $40-$60

Homemade box .... $5-$20

⁓ If you don't have room or enough keepsakes for a memorabilia box, make your own wedding scrapbook instead. Again, you'll do better to make your own rather than to buy one in a bridal store. You can keep all the notes, swatches, samples of perfume, and pictures you'll treasure years from now in this book.

COMPARE AND SAVE

Store-bought bridal scrapbook .... $20-$30

Homemade bridal scrapbook .... $10-$15

⁓ Save copies of the letters you've written to update your bridal party and the letters you and your fiancé have written to one another during the planning of your wedding. No need for those specially ordered computer-printed love notes you can buy through catalogs. The real thing will do fine.

~ If your photo–developing store offers double prints for the same price as singles, or a free enlargement, take the opportunity to save money on prints you'd otherwise have to make for relatives and friends anyway.

HIGH-TECH SAVINGS

Some brides are going the high-tech route with their keepsakes by choosing to have their favorite wedding portrait transferred onto a floppy disk or scanned into their computer, and then sent electronically to all of their distant friends and relatives. Hint: get a friend with a great computer system to do the scanning for you; then you don't have to pay fifteen dollars at a photo shop. With a good photo-editing program that comes standard with many computers now, you can play with borders, artwork, clips, fonts, and more. Many brides recommend this as an inexpensive (practically free) way to send a snapshot to everyone on your list in an amazingly short amount of time.

Of course, non–computer-friendly relatives and friends can still get regular photos in the mail.

～ Printed napkins and matchboxes are keepsakes that can be cut out. If you find these nonessentials necessary, however, take extra care to comparison shop in discount stationery stores and at print shops to get the best bargain possible. Include in your price research those items that may be offered by the reception hall as well. In some instances, they may even be offered as freebies. Check well.

18

How Many Guests?

Size does matter when it comes to per-guest expenses. Everything from the location to the meals and drinks served depends on the head count of your guests. There's no need to try to save money by slicing your guest list to pieces and alienating half of the people you know. With some smart planning you can work your guest list to give you the opportunity to spend less on your wedding.

∼ Make it clear that the guest limits for each side are firm numbers so that neither side overextends, thinking they can just slide by. Make it known how serious you are and you'll avoid the tensions of overstepped boundaries. Too many brides have been pushed into accepting "just three more" over and over—and at fifty to one hundred fifty dollars per person, the figures add up.

〜 If you have to invite many guests, plan a more informal reception to reduce the cost of meals per person.

〜 Once the lists are drawn, go down each column marking "definites" and "maybes." You'll know better where to begin your cuts should your original guest-list numbers be too high for your budget. Obviously, the fewer guests you invite, the less you'll have to pay for your reception. However, don't make your guest list too small. You'll insult relatives and friends by excluding them, and you'll also feel that you've ripped yourself off when there's next to nobody passing through the receiving line. Just work toward a fair and comfortable medium.

〜 Consider excluding children. With the wording of your invitation, you're aware, you indicate to your guests that their children are not invited to the wedding. When you're paying one hundred dollars per person, it makes sense to leave out the fifteen toddlers and infants who won't even eat their very expensive meals. Yes, many formal halls count each body present as a full-price person. Ask the manager of your location if this is the case.

〜 Don't allow teenagers and uncommitted daters to bring uninvited guests to your wedding. This will be evident in the wording of the invitation, but if a person indicates to you that she's planning to bring a date, it's your right to remind her that space limitations prevent you from letting her bring a guest. Tell her how your sister, the maid of honor, isn't even bringing a guest. If a response card is returned to you with a written-in addition of a guest's escort (an entirely inappropriate move not cleared with you first), call the offender and tactfully remind him or her that space on the guest list does not allow additional people to be invited to the wedding. Don't be manipulated into paying for this extra person when your college roommates, your boss, and your second cousins all had to be left off the list.

～ If you have many relatives, friends, and clients you just won't be able to invite to the wedding, plan an additional party for them either a week before the wedding or after your return from your honeymoon. Make it clear that no gifts are necessary, so that no charges of greed are leveled against you. The important thing is to celebrate with your closest acquaintances.

～ When looking at price per head, keep in mind that you may have to feed the entertainment. A DJ is only one person and only one price, while a full band may cost you twelve full meals. It's best to keep the numbers low.

～ When expenses look like they could start getting out of hand, it's time to start cutting the guest list. Begin with those marked as "maybes."

~ Cut those guests who have drifted from you in the past few months and years.

~ Cut old high school and college friends you're sure you'll never see again.

~ Cut people you're inviting simply because you were invited to their wedding fifteen years ago, but you haven't seen or spoken to more than three times since.

~ Cut your parents' friends and clients who don't really know you.

~ Cut a whole level of guests—such as all second cousins.

~ Ask the groom's family to cut their guests equally. This is tough to do, so compromise as much as possible.

~ Don't send invitations to faraway relatives with the idea that they won't be able to make it but you're sending the invitation to be nice. They might decide to hop a plane and attend after all; then you have to add on a handful of guests you hadn't counted on. One bride was shocked when overseas relatives responded that all ten of them would attend her wedding. Her advice: "Be careful who you invite; they just may show up."

19

Invitations

Invitations, response cards, and programs can add up to a large part of your wedding budget. You can cut the expense without sending a cheap-looking, tacky invitation to your guests by knowing the details of the invitation-printing business and making the right selection. Remember, your invitations reflect the formality and style of your wedding, giving your guests an idea of what to expect and how to dress for the occasion. Design your invitation packages with that in mind, so you're not tempted to commit a faux pas by selecting the wrong invitation just to save money.

∼ The formality of your wedding is reflected in your invitations. So choose invitations that match the style of your wedding. Even formal invitations can still be found for bargain prices.

INVITATION RESOURCES

American Stationery Company—800-822-2577

American Wedding Album—800-428-0379

Anna Griffin Invitation Design—404-817-8170,
www.annagriffin.com

Botanical PaperWorks—888-727-3755,
www.BotanicalPaperWorks.com

Camelot Wedding Stationery—800-280-2860

Carlson Craft—507-625-0879

Cranes—800-572-0024

Embossed Graphics—800-325-1016,
www.embossedgraphics.com

Envelopments—800-335-3536

Invitations by Dawn—800-332-3296

Jamie Lee Fine—800-288-5800

Julie Holcomb Printers—510-654-6416,
www.julieholcombprinters.com

Now and Forever—800-521-0584

PaperStyle.com (ordering invitations on-line)—770-667-6100,
www.paperstyle.com

Papyrus—800-886-6700, www.papyrusonline.com

The Precious Collection—800-537-5222

Renaissance Writings—800-246-8483,
www.renaissancewriting.com

Rexcraft—800-635-3898

〜 Know exactly how many invitations you will need so you can comparison shop with the applicable numbers.

〜 As you already know, shop around in several different stationery stores to get the best prices available. Comparison shop like crazy. Send for free catalogs.

〜 When adding up the number of invitations you'll need, follow these rules: families get their own; those over the age of eighteen get their own; and those inviting a guest get one invitation with both names on it (no need for a separate invitation for the guest).

〜 Plan to order ten to fifteen extras in case of mistakes or replacement guests added to the list when space allows. Leftovers may be kept as mementos.

〜 When figuring your invitation budget, be sure to add in the cost of postage. The two expenses go hand in hand. In most cases, you'll need two first-class stamps per invitation. If your invitation is oversized, of heavy paper stock, or includes many inserts, it may require extra postage on the outer envelope. International rates are higher. Don't guess. Take one invitation to the post office and have them weigh it.

〜 Take several of those large invitation sample books home with you so you can take a really good look through them and compare prices.

〜 Choose simple, plain, black-and-white invitations rather than the more expensive, fancier ones. Colored inks, borders, pictures, monograms, and laser-cut designs just inflate the price. As an added benefit, the simpler the invitations, the classier they look.

〜 Choose thermographed invitations rather than engraved. You won't see much of a difference in style, but they're a much better buy. Linda Zec of An Invitation to Buy–Nationwide says thermographed invitations can cost up to 50 percent less than engraved ones.

〜 Get regular- to small-sized invitations. They're less expensive than oversized ones, and extra postage is not needed for each one.

〜 Get plain envelopes. The colored ones with the printed and shiny liners are all decoration and all added expense.

〜 Choose invitations that are made of thinner paper so you'll pay less in postage.

∼ When looking at catalog prices for invitation packages, be sure to add on the cost of shipping and insurance.

∼ Word your order form carefully and edit several times to check for mistakes. One misspelled word can mean the extra expense of having to reorder if the catalog's low prices mean no returns.

∼ Rather than order professional invitations from a printer or a catalog, you could choose to make your own, using good paper and your high-quality computer and printer. Today's paper and stationery stores stock a wide selection of beautiful bridal-themed invitation card stock, papers, and envelopes for you to use. Carefully follow the wording and patterns you see on invitations in wedding books and magazines, and enclose these in high-quality, matching envelopes with response cards. Or, make use of a friend's computer skills and software. This favor can be a wedding gift to you.

∼ Speaking of the cost of materials, buy your own white or off-white paper at a discount store or in one of those buy-by-the-pound paper warehouses. Get your plain envelopes there, too, remembering that colored papers are generally more expensive than the preferable white and off-white varieties.

PAPER PRODUCT RESOURCES

OfficeMax—check your local listings

Paper Access—800-727-3701, www.paperaccess.com

Paper Direct—800-A-PAPERS, www.paperdirect.com

Rexcraft—888-796-1184

Staples—www.staples.com

Ultimate Wedding Store—www.ultimatewedding.com/store

The Wedding Store—www.wedguide.com/store

Weddingware—800-622-4489

Wedmart.com—888-802-2229, www.wedmart.com

≈ If you have connections to an art school, perhaps you'd trust tomorrow's designers to create your invitations for you. Their fee will be reasonable, undoubtedly little more than the cost of materials and a request for referrals.

≈ Another alternative: use your computer to draw up the invitation you'd like, and bring a crisp printout to a nearby discount printer to be copied as many times as you need. While it's not as much of a savings as printing the invitations yourself, it's still less expensive than the professionally printed ones, and you're likely to get outstanding quality.

∼ If you have experience in calligraphy, hand-print a master copy of your invitation. Then either bring this master copy to a discount printer to be duplicated or, if you have the time and patience, you can hand-print all your invitations in calligraphy. It's a classy look if you have the talent, and it's more than a bargain.

CALLIGRAPHY RESOURCE

Petals and Ink—818-509-6783, www.petalsnink.com

∼ If you'd like the look of calligraphy for your invitations, ask an artist friend to write out your invitation as his gift to you. Or put up a flyer at a local high school or college art department, asking for the services of a calligrapher. Many young artists are just as talented as professionals, and they'd gladly do the job for a fraction of a professional's fee. They also use the work for their portfolios.

∼ Professional calligraphers charge substantial fees for their work, so if you must hire out the job, comparison shop for the best talent at the right price.

COMPARE AND SAVE

Professional calligrapher .... $100 and up

Do it yourself .... $25 for supplies

A friend's gift to you .... free

∽ Don't order your invitations too early—there may be a last-minute change of date, time, or place. Most brides do well to order their invitations four to six months in advance. By then, everything should be fairly well finalized.

∽ When placing your order, print all information carefully, double-check, have your fiancé double-check, and then check again. Any mistakes you've made in the order will be printed on your invitation, and you'll be stuck with them.

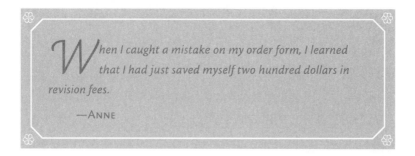

When I caught a mistake on my order form, I learned that I had just saved myself two hundred dollars in revision fees.

—ANNE

∼ Make sure there's a return policy in your contract in case there is a mistake in the printing of the invitations or damage to your order in shipping.

∼ Keep all receipts as proof of purchase, and get the sales-person's name when you place your order. Other information you should record: date of your order, specifics about the style and amount you're ordering, changes, delivery date, amount of deposit, and further payment obligations. These steps help in case of questions.

∼ Check your invitations carefully when you go to pick them up. If you find mistakes right away, your chances are bet-ter for getting them corrected and compensated.

∼ Don't try to save a few dollars by not ordering response cards with your invitations. They're the best way to keep a record of how many guests will be in attendance at your wed-ding. You don't want to have to total up your guest list by *call-ing* all your relatives and friends.

∼ Mail the invitations early enough so that the response cards will be returned to you several weeks before you have to give the final head count to the caterer. A delay or change could cost you money.

> ## POSTAL SERVICE ON-LINE
>
> *To save time and make sure your invitations reach your guests, visit the U.S. Postal Service's website at www.usps.gov/welcome .htm. Here, you can order "Love" stamps (for a few extra dollars for delivery) and easily look up zip codes for your guests' home-towns. However, don't use the Internet to get an old friend's address since these listings are sometimes out of date. Give your friend a quick call and ask for the address.*

~ Be sure you have all your guests' names and addresses correct so no invitations are returned to you, leaving an irate aunt who thinks she has been snubbed.

At-Home Cards

~ Separate cards to announce your permanent address, phone number, and even the name you'll be assuming (whether it's his, yours, or a hyphenated combination) are one of those nonessentials that can easily be cut to keep your wedding and postage costs down, especially if your guests already know where you'll be living. This information can be printed on the back of your wedding program.

*T*hank-You Notes

~ Rather than order these with your invitations as part of your stationery package, simply use a high-quality plain stationery (not necessarily thank-you or bride's stationery), and hand-write your thank-you in black ink. Comparison shop among discount stationery stores for the best price, taking care to look at price-per-card cost.

~ Just phoning or printing form-letter thank-yous out on your computer may seem like a savings, but they're actually grievous don'ts in the etiquette world. Just the same, don't use those boxed, fill-in-the-blank thank-you cards. They're not only expensive, they're tacky.

*M*aps

~ If you're planning to send maps to your guests who might need help finding the ceremony site and the location of the reception, include the directions with the invitation. There's no sense in sending them separately. Draw your own map or create one on your computer for clear directions, then check them well for changes or confusing routes. At one wedding recently, many guests missed the ceremony and arrived just in time for the reception due to the map's omission of a confusing traffic circle.

〜 Many hotels and reception halls provide printed maps and directions to their sites. In most cases, these thorough direction sheets are free for the asking.

〜 Copy your map or directions on a photocopier—yours, a friend's, or the one at work—any one you can use for free. An added tip: reduce these maps so you can fit two to four to each page. Then copy these sheets at less of a strain on paper or supplies or on your cash supply if you have to pay to use a copier.

〜 Of course, send maps only to those guests who need them, as well as to your vendors.

20

Legal Matters

The licenses and paperwork are more than just technicalities of your wedding. They can also add up to quite an expense. Learn how to avoid extra fees by handling your legal affairs in the best possible manner.

⌁ Believe it or not, it may be more expensive to get your blood tests done in some places than in others. So forget about the doctor's office and the twenty-four-hour clinic if they plan to charge you, and look around for a free place like a clinic or medical school. At the very least, comparison shop for the best price. One bride saved thirty dollars through her research in this area. A document is a document, no matter where the test is taken.

〜 Make sure you have your blood test done at the appropriate time. Depending on your state's rules, these tests are valid only for a certain amount of time. If you miss the window, you'll have to pay to have another done within the allotted time. Also, allow enough time to receive your test results. Many officiants will not sign the needed paperwork for your wedding without these.

〜 Schedule your blood tests, if they're required by your state, to coincide with your regular yearly physical. Just be sure to inform your doctor so he or she can tell you about any rules, regulations, or special tests you'll need. Combining this physical with your annual one can save you up to two hundred dollars in office visit fees in some areas. While you're there, get your immunization shots required for honeymoon travel in some exotic regions.

〜 You may be considering writing up a prenuptial agreement. While it may seem a good idea to just write your wishes down and put them in a safe place, your state will require much more legal documentation than that. Consult a legal directory in your library, or place a call to a free legal advice center in your area.

〜 Invest in a good lawyer to help you prepare solid, well-written, and complete prenuptial agreements that protect your interests. Taking this step now may save you a lot of money down the line. Legal experts advise, though, that for your agreement to stand up in court, it cannot be signed too close to the wedding date. A judge might find that you or your partner felt coerced into signing and the agreement would be thrown out in court. Have a rational discussion with your partner about your feelings and wishes regarding the prenup and take smart legal steps for your protection.

~ Just like the blood tests, your marriage license is only valid for a certain amount of time. So make sure your ceremony will take place in time, and make sure you can get your marriage license in time. For instance, don't apply for it the day before your wedding. Some states require a twenty-four-hour or longer processing time.

~ Check with your local wedding license registrar at town hall for a printed copy of all of your state's marriage license requirements. Laws change often and even websites may have incorrect information regarding required tests, waiting periods, and courses needed. Having a printed copy of the rules will help prevent you from following old laws, paying extra for retesting after an expired validity time, or from not being allowed to marry due to missed blood tests and the like.

NAME CHANGE

If you're planning to take your fiancé's name or hyphenate your own with his, you have some paperwork to fill out. It may not cost anything to change your name on important documents and accounts, but it could cost you plenty in the long run if your official documents are not amended. So be sure to call, write, or otherwise arrange your name change in the following:

Social Security number
Driver's license
Credit cards
Bank and loan accounts
On-line accounts
Investment accounts
Passport
Stocks and bonds
Expense accounts
Telephone cards
Telephone account
Cell phone and pager
  accounts

Subscriptions
Medical records
Prescriptions
Professional
  associations
School records and
  alumni associations
Other billing accounts
Other forms of ID
Library cards
Airline frequent flier
  programs

~ In addition, you and your partner should have your insurance policies and wills updated to accommodate the change in your lives. In the long run, you'll save time and money by tending to this now.

~ Let a special relative know that her engagement gift to you was used to pay for your marriage license. That can be a special thrill for the giver, particularly if she originally introduced the two of you or is in any way responsible for your getting married.

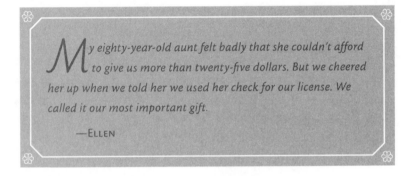

My eighty-year-old aunt felt badly that she couldn't afford to give us more than twenty-five dollars. But we cheered her up when we told her we used her check for our license. We called it our most important gift.

—Ellen

21

The Rings

These are the most lasting symbols of your wedding day and a state-ment of your personal style. Since platinum is by far the most popular wedding ring choice today, you'll have a hard time finding rock-bottom prices without compromising quality. While you shouldn't try to take too many shortcuts in saving on your bands, there are ways to get the best value and insure them for less.

Where to Find Your Rings

∼ Look in magazines or brochures to get an idea of the kinds of rings you want. It's best to have a general idea before you walk into a jewelry store so you won't be swayed by the flashy choices in the display cabinet or by the commission-motivated salesclerk.

∼ Before you start your hunt, do some research on what to look for in quality gold and precious-gem jewelry. Diamonds, for instance, are priced according to carat, color, clarity, and cut. You'll want to know which specifications of each warrant the higher prices. Bridal magazines often run articles on how to buy a diamond, and you can get literature on the subject from a good jewelry store or on a wedding ring information website such as the Amercian Gem Society's (www.ags.org).

∼ Because platinum is all the rage now for its shine, durability, and value, you will find that its prices are lofty. To shop well and get the best your money can buy, contact the Platinum Guild International USA at 949-760-8279 for literature on buying platinum.

∼ Bring along a relative or friend who knows something about jewelry when you're shopping. You'll be more likely to ask the right questions.

∼ Ring stores in the mall may at times offer competitive prices during sales; in general, though, their prices will figure in location rental and upkeep fees. Their prime spot in the mall could mean less savings on retail prices.

~ For great deals on quality gems, shop in the diamond district of your nearest major city. This is where the buyers for all of those jewelry stores in the mall come to get wholesale prices and then sell the same jewels to you at higher prices. Check out where they're shopping and you may discover a great find.

~ Go to your family's regular jeweler for proven reliability and a possible discount for your loyalty to the place. One bride received 10 percent off on her rings just because she'd recently bought a gift there for her mother.

~ Comparison shop for your rings in different stores of different sizes, in different parts of town. Price tags vary, and you may be able to find a great deal.

~ Check discount jewelry stores and department stores. Sales flyers will announce special savings, and throughout-the-store discounts may apply at the jewelry counter.

~ If you have a friend in the business, see if you can use his or her employee discount to garner a better price for your rings. This of course takes a good friend, who will be giving up a slice of commission on your purchase. It's worth a shot.

〜 Keep an eye out for sales, clearances, and specials. Ask your family and bridal party to watch for specials in stores near them as well. It could mean savings of 10 percent or more, which could translate into a sizable discount. The pre-Christmas and post–Valentine's Day sales offer amazing price cuts.

〜 Ask your friends and family for referrals to the stores where they bought their rings.

〜 If the store isn't a large one, part of a national chain or well-known line, check it out with the Better Business Bureau to see if it's legitimate or if any charges have been leveled against it. A ring purchase is a large-ticket item, so your best bet is to protect your investment—even before you make it.

〜 Part of your criteria for choosing a ring shop is its engraving and sizing policies. If both are included free—and in some places they aren't—it's an advantage. Measure this one carefully, though, because an expensive store with free sizing and engraving is not better than an inexpensive store that charges extra for engraving and sizing.

Ring Information and Company Websites

American Gem Society (for information on buying quality rings)—800-346-8485, www.ags.org

Benchmark—800-633-5950, www.benchmarkrings.com

Bianca—213-622-7234, www.BiancaPlatinum.com

DeBeers—www.adiamondisforever.com

Diamond Information Society—www.adiamondisforever.com

EGL Gemological Society—877-EGL-USA-1, EGLUSA@worldnet.att.net

Honora—888-2HONORA

Keepsake Diamond Jewelry—888-4-KEEPSAKE

Novell—888-916-6835, www.novelldesignstudio.com

OGI Wedding Bands Unlimited—800-578-3846, www.ogi-ltd.com

Paul Klecka—888-P-KLECKA, www.klecka.com

Platinum Guild International USA—949-760-8279, www.preciousplatinum.com

Rudolf Erdel Platinum—212-633-9333, www.rudolferdel.com

Scott Kay Platinum—800-487-4898, www.scottkay.com

Platinum is enjoying renewed popularity. But it is the most expensive precious metal out there, so be prepared to shell out thousands for a beautiful platinum ring. Most brides say it's worth the investment, and this is one place where you should not be cheap.

For information on how to design your own rings, which could be a savings if you do it right, check out www.adiamondis forever.com.

〜 Consider buying your rings in an antique shop, where beautiful rings with some history are offered at lower prices. Just be sure to get the rings appraised immediately to be sure you've gotten your money's worth. You may even find that your fifty-dollar ring is actually a valuable piece of jewelry.

〜 No matter where you're ordering your rings, the choices you make can save you some money. Choose a set of plain rings over the swirly, gaudy ones that are larger than your whole hand . . . for obvious reasons. Another plus for smaller, simpler rings without texture and braiding is that they have no ridges to catch dirt, so they're easier to keep clean.

〜 Buy plain gold bands rather than the kinds with the set stones.

〜 Make sure you're getting your money's worth. Check the inside of the bands for a fourteen-carat (14k) gold marking if that's what you're buying.

〜 Economical choices may be gold- or silver-plated bands. They still carry the same meaning, no matter what they're made of.

⌣ Compare the prices of his and hers wedding band sets to the prices of individual rings. Only in that way can you decide which is the better buy. Some sets on sale can save you up to a hundred dollars off the price of individual rings.

⌣ If you know someone who makes jewelry as a hobby, commission that person to make your rings for you. No doubt the cost will be much lower than a store's, and your friend will be given a great honor. You also may design your own rings. Jillian found it special to actually help create her and her fiancé's wedding bands. She designed the rings, then helped a friend make them. In doing so, she saved two hundred fifty dollars.

⌣ Put up flyers at a local art school or college with a jewelry workshop regarding your search for an artist to make a set of wedding rings. Students love these opportunities for their portfolios and independent study projects, and you'll undoubtedly get the ring for little more than the cost of materials. That can be more than half off store prices.

⌣ Look into the talents and prices of local crafters for custom-made rings at discount prices. Comparison shop among these artists as well.

⌒ For the ultimate savings and meaning, exchange rings handed down to you by relatives. Keeping the bands in the family is important, and it's a special tie to those who have worn the bands before you.

⌒ Have the stones from an heirloom ring set in your wedding band. You save money on them, and the inclusion of your grandmother's diamonds in your ring is a very special gesture.

⌒ Buy stones separately from a discount supplier; then have them set into a ring you've gotten a bargain on elsewhere. The savings here: fifty to two hundred dollars.

⌒ Don't fall for those too-good-to-be-true ring sales in odd locations—like the back of a van. Only shop at reputable jewelers, and remember, if it seems too good to be true, it probably is.

*P*ayment

⌒ Get a written appraisal of your rings with your receipt.

⌒ Make sure your ring supplier offers a good return policy, in case you must exchange them for another size or style.

⇝ A good warranty should be offered to you as well. Ask about it.

⇝ Think seriously about whether you want to arrange an installment plan for paying off your rings. Interest will pile up, costing you much more money than the price of the ring. A better alternative is to use your credit card—ensuring you proper reimbursement in case of a problem and, at times, credits or frequent flier miles. Just be sure to pay off that amount on your credit card with some of your wedding gift money so you're not accumulating interest on your credit account.

After the Purchase

⇝ After you buy your rings, have them appraised immediately. Go to a jeweler other than the one from whom you bought the ring for this service (why would the salesclerk want you to know your ring isn't really worth the eight hundred dollars your fiancé spent?).

⇝ Have your rings insured immediately. In case of loss or theft, you'll be reimbursed their full value. The American Gem Society offers a great free brochure on the details of insuring your rings.

〜 Store your rings in a safe or lockbox at home before the wedding—just don't store them so safely away that you forget where they are.

〜 On the night before the wedding, leave a note on your door to take the rings with you when you leave for the ceremony!

22

Flowers and Decorations

Brides who have tried too hard to save money in this area report that they regretted settling for less than they wanted for their wedding day. You don't have to shortchange your floral vision for the sake of saving money. Here you'll find out how to get more for your flower budget by making the right choices according to style, season, and selection.

~ Check with the officiant or the manager of the site of the wedding. Will the location be decorated already? If so, you have much less to buy. One bride learned that her church would be decorated already with poinsettias and white candles on the date of her pre-Christmas wedding. This saved her five hundred dollars in extra florist fees.

~ Another reason to check with the officiant at a church or synagogue is to inquire about rules regarding decoration. You may not be allowed to set up pew arrangements, and it would be unfortunate to find this out after you paid seventy-five dollars for yours. You should get the dos and don'ts before you start ordering.

~ See if there will be other weddings taking place at your wedding location on the same day as yours. Perhaps you could arrange through the officiant or manager to share basic decorations with the other bride or brides at a savings to all of you. Emily asked the officiant to give her name to the other bride, who then contacted her. They saved two hundred dollars by splitting the costs of decorating their church.

~ Set a budget for your flowers, using the figures you've discovered through introductory research or talks with recently married friends, and stick to it.

*W*here to Look

~ Don't go to a big, fancy florist connected to a bridal salon, a mall, a hotel, or even a caterer. Their elevated prices mean you're also paying for their rent, their facilities, their advertising, and their larger staff. Instead, look at a more moderate supplier.

∼ Use your family's regular florist because you're sure of their reliability and quality of service. You may even get a discount for being a regular customer. Karen received a 20 percent discount on her wedding flowers from her regular florist, plus another 10 percent off because the same florist also did her sister's wedding.

∼ Check wholesalers in your area. Their prices are by nature lower than those you'll find in other stores and markets. You'll find listings of these in the Yellow Pages.

∼ Comparison shop at several different florists and nurseries in several different parts of town. Prices may vary depending on neighborhood, access, size of facilities, and type of clientele. Of course, suburban shops tend to be less expensive than urban ones, but the added price of travel and transport could cancel out that discount, so search out the best areas at the least expense to you.

∼ A shop that grows its flowers and plants on-site is generally less expensive than the shop that has to have all of its blooms shipped in. So look for greenhouse or gardening space around the shops you're checking out.

~ Ask your nearby friends and relatives if they would suggest a florist whose service they liked. Use that information when you're comparing prices and packages.

~ Find a young, just-starting-out-in-the-business florist who will give his or her all. Most often, these beginners lack experience, not talent, and their reasonable prices are meant to attract accounts that will give them valuable exposure. Tracy found a great new florist at considerable savings when a hard-working newcomer distributed flyers at the market. So don't count out the young ones. You just might get a great deal.

~ When comparison shopping at floral suppliers, review their brochures and sample albums and ask to see arrangements they're working on now. Note their prices and the elements of their packages so that you can compare and contrast all the possibilities.

When ordering, keep the following things in mind to save yourself some money.

∽ Get a price comparison chart for each of the flowers you might want to include in your bouquets and decorations. This way, you'll be able to see which blooms are most and least expensive, and you can choose the most economical ones. Lilies, carnations, and freesia, for example, are far less costly choices than the popular stephanotis and orchids.

∽ Use the florist's chart as well to find out which flowers have to be flown in. Shipping an exotic selection of flowers will be more expensive than those found closer.

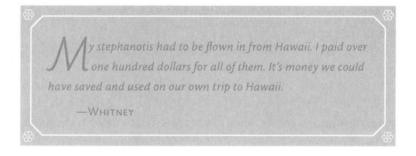

My stephanotis had to be flown in from Hawaii. I paid over one hundred dollars for all of them. It's money we could have saved and used on our own trip to Hawaii.

—WHITNEY

∽ Order flowers that are in season. Just like fruits and vegetables, prices go up when it's not their prime time. Your florist can tell you what will be in season on your wedding day.

∽ You don't have to buy the cheapest flowers available. According to Marilyn Waga of Belle Fleur in New York City,

"Use a few great, eye-catching flowers in each arrangement, rather than a lot of unimpressive, cheap flowers." Great, beautiful blooms can be just as lovely as a bunch of roses, and it will make your bouquet more original.

〜 Order the more popular flowers like carnations and baby roses. They're usually the least expensive and most appropriate choices.

〜 Use traditional wedding flowers sparingly, especially during the most popular wedding months like June and September. White roses, stephanotis, gardenias, and orange blossoms are more expensive then.

〜 Inexpensive flowers that work well in any floral arrangement are ivy (which symbolizes wedded bliss), gerbera daisies, zinnias in bright colors, tulips in season, leatherleaf, and Queen Anne's lace.

〜 Order miniature flowers rather than the full-sized variety. Not only are they more delicate, they may be priced at a fraction of the cost—depending on the particular flower.

〜 Consider sprays, which have several flowers per sprig. One spray can give the appearance of several three-dollar flowers.

∽ Use color in your bouquets and arrangements. A splash of color gives the impression of more flowers in the bunch, and you won't have to buy as many flowers to make a statement as if you used all-white arrangements.

∽ Use more greenery in your bouquets and decorations. The natural look is in, so include plenty of ferns and pretty leaves to fill out a bouquet with fewer flowers.

∽ Consider filling out your bouquets and decorations with Queen Anne's lace or similar inexpensive blooms.

∽ A more economical choice is to order the greenery, such as ferns and fillers from the florist, but pick your own flowers from your garden. You can easily incorporate the flowers into your bouquet. Renée saved an amazing six hundred dollars this way, and it was special for her to carry in her bouquet the flowers she and her fiancé had planted together. Even actress Kellie Martin, formerly on *ER*, chose this option for her bouquet.

∽ Be sure the shape of your bouquet fits your height and size. A short bride looks hidden behind a too-large bouquet, so avoid ordering a more expensive style that isn't right for you.

〜 Big bouquets are out. The current styles favor smaller nosegay or Biedermeier styles that still make a lovely bouquet but use fewer flowers. Plus, smaller brides get lost behind a large bouquet, and the cut and details of your gown will be hidden on the way down the aisle.

〜 Order a much smaller bouquet for the one you'll toss to the waiting single women at your reception. There is no rule that says it has to be identical to your real one. Or you could just toss your own bouquet if you're not planning to preserve it and keep it as a memento of your day. Also, the bouquet toss is falling out of fashion, so you may want to skip ordering a nosegay.

〜 Corsages to be worn by the mothers and grandmothers don't have to be very large. In fact, most women would prefer a smaller corsage to wear on the wedding day. Check if corsages worn on the wrist are less expensive than the pin-on variety at your floral designer's.

〜 Rather than order flowered hair clips for your bridesmaids, plan to snip some baby's breath from bouquets or even from your garden to adorn their hair. Your savings here, depending on the style, could reach a hundred dollars.

∾ Before ordering a white aisle runner from your florist, check to see if the church or wedding location has one or simply skip the aisle runner. You'll look better in contrast with a darker floor rather than blending with a white path. An off-white dress will look better, too, without the white clash underfoot.

∾ If your wedding location is already nicely decorated, you could skip the pew decorations. If your first several rows need to be reserved with some kind of markers, use lengths of ribbon instead of decorations. Craft stores offer inexpensive pew bow kits for under ten dollars.

Delivery

∾ Bypass the delivery fee and pick up your order from the florist yourself. You could save twenty-five to fifty dollars, depending on the size of your order. Make sure you have plenty of insulated coolers and sturdy boxes so that your flowers will arrive fresh and uncrushed at the wedding.

∾ Of course, if you'll be picking up the flowers yourself, you'll want to arrange to do it at the last possible time before the ceremony. It could be a morning run after breakfast, or you could send someone from your bridal party in your place.

∼ Decorating the ceremony and reception locations with these freshly picked-up supplies is another wedding morning task that might be best handled by a less-nervous bridal attendant or helpful friends and relatives.

∼ You can make your own chuppah (for your Jewish wedding) with flowers and garlands from your garden. Again, consult how-to books, or just model yours after those you've seen.

∼ Instead of ordering rose petals to be strewn about by the flower girl during the ceremony, gently pull the petals off several roses from your garden. One bride who followed this tip saved seventy-five dollars on her florist bill.

∼ Use candelabras or candleholders from your home. If you were to rent these for several tables, you could spend anywhere from fifty to seventy-five dollars.

∼ If your wedding falls in the right season, cut evergreens from your Christmas tree before you discard it. Unsold Christmas trees may be purchased after the season for a minimal price. Use the branches as centerpiece additions.

～ Use potted plants from home or borrow potted plants and flowering bushes from friends and family to decorate your reception.

～ Buy your centerpieces as investments in your future home. Home Depot's selection of topiaries in pretty clay pots can be set out on each table. After the wedding have a friend bring them back to your house to use as home or garden decor. If you want flowers rather than greenery, here's a great secret shared by a bride in Kentucky: go to your local upscale supermarket and raid its flower section of all the potted flowering plants. This bride bought thirty potted plants for ninety dollars and kept the colored foil paper on the flowerpots for a bright look.

～ Cut branches from flowering trees as decoration for your tables, buffet tables, and the altar. Again, this must be done shortly before the ceremony so your blooms aren't wilting and discoloring. Keep cut branches cool and their angle-cut stems in water.

～ For a head table or buffet table, use a good tablecloth from home rather than renting one.

~ Buy candles in bulk from discount stores, craft supply houses, even catalogs. And freeze them before using them— they'll last much longer.

Centerpieces

There's no need for expensive florist-created centerpieces. Oversized ones obstruct your guests' view of one another (and you) anyway, and a pretty centerpiece doesn't necessarily have to have a large price tag attached. Here are some inexpensive alternatives to the tabletop jungle.

~ Arrange candles of different heights and one color (white may be the least expensive) to create a romantic look for each table. Remember to freeze the candles first so they will burn more slowly.

~ Set in the center of each table groups of framed pictures of you and your fiancé together, with family, with friends, as children, and so on. Use the frames and pictures you've taken from your own walls and countertops, and recruit both families to bring theirs in as well. (Ask them to stick an address label on the backs of their frames for easier return after the party.) One bride found that her guests loved looking at the photos on the table; they were appreciated far more than one hundred dollars' worth of floral centerpieces would have been.

∼ Float miniature candles along with flower petals in a large water-filled glass bowl at the center of each table. You can use your own—or borrow—large glass bowls, and then pick the flower petals from your backyard blooms. The cost here for a very classy look: under fifty dollars.

∼ Arrange a fruit bowl at the center of each table or place a larger one as the centerpiece of a buffet table. Search farmer's markets and supermarkets for the best quality and prices available, or ask the reception hall manager if the fruit from the buffet table might be arranged this way.

∼ A large bread basket makes a great centerpiece, especially if you include braided breads and a variation of shapes, sizes, and colors. Again, ask the caterer if you'd be able to use the bread intended for the buffet table for this purpose. Use your own pretty baskets or borrow them. If baskets are not available to you, simply cover any kind of bowl with a large cloth napkin and have it drape over the bowl once it's filled with rolls. (In days long ago, grain was considered a symbol of fertility, and the bride and groom were showered with grain for that very reason. In other cultures of the past, bread was a gift brought by all and arranged in one pile. This is thought to be the origin of the wedding cake.)

~ Neatly arranged groups of wedding favors also make nice centerpieces. Why not get double duty out of your favors and save some money at the same time?

~ Check markets, sales, even your attic for items you can use as centerpieces. A brass theme will allow you to dig up all sorts of interesting things.

~ Choose creative centerpieces rather than floral arrangements. For a holiday wedding, set out pretty bowls or silver trays filled with a selection of your holiday ornaments. For a beach wedding, fill a small fishbowl with sand, some seashells, and starfish.

Consider the following ideas if you're not the do-it-yourself type but want the do-it-yourself savings.

~ Contact a floral design college or school to request their services as a group project for pay. The instructor will surely jump at your offer, and you'll wind up paying much less than you would to a commercial business. The quality is often outstanding, as these students are fresh in their knowledge of technique and the rules of design.

∽ Accept the services of an experienced relative or friend as his or her wedding gift to you.

∽ To fill your hall or tent with lights, ask your relatives if you can borrow their strings of white Christmas lights. Label each string with the lender's name, and then use all of the strings together to create a lovely, starry look for your site.

23

Transportation for All

The most important thing on the wedding day is actually getting to the ceremony and reception. You will want to arrive and depart in style, so learn here how to book transportation for less and avoid extra fees that can wreck a budget.

$\mathcal{F}$or the Bride and Groom

~ When looking for limousines, always comparison shop. Prices vary *wildly*, and certain companies offer special packages and discounts. Make plenty of calls and take plenty of notes. Of course, you'll need to know your wedding date when you start looking for a limo company—some agencies may not have any limousines available on your wedding day.

⌒ Never contract with a limousine agency with just a phone call. Always go to see the cars. You want to be sure you won't wind up with an old red model with a worn interior and no air-conditioning—their version of "deluxe."

⌒ Contact the National Limousine Association at 800–NLA–7007 for resources and to check the track record of the limousine companies that interest you.

⌒ Ask what the drivers will be wearing. A reputable agency will have their drivers in suits or tuxedos.

⌒ When adding up the number of limousines needed, you can cut costs tremendously by just getting one for yourselves. After all, the bridal party doesn't have to be transported in limos.

⌒ Figure out how many cars you really need. One limousine company owner told me that he regularly has to decrease couples' estimates of the number of cars needed to transport their guests. Don't forget that some limousines seat eight, some seat ten, and some seat twelve or more.

⌒ Choose a regular, not a stretch, limousine for the two of you. The look is the same, but the price is lower.

〜 Choose a black limousine rather than a white one. White limos are far more expensive than the standard black ones, which gives you a better deal and more availability when shopping for your wedding day ride.

〜 Pass on the special bridal package that includes a complimentary bottle of champagne for the bride and groom. Most brides who paid for this type of package said either the champagne wasn't very good or the church and reception hall were so close that they didn't have any time to drink the champagne. Just a plain old ride in the car will do.

〜 Ask for the free extras that are now becoming standard in the transportation industry: red carpet leading up to the car door; champagne stand for a post-ceremony champagne toast by the car; water, ice, and snacks stocked in the limousine. Don't allow a company to charge you extra for any of these items. They're free at most reputable companies.

〜 Be sure to schedule your time wisely. If you keep the limousine driver waiting outside the reception hall for you to leave the party—and you've stayed an hour longer than you planned to because you were having so much fun—you could wind up paying the driver for the extra time *plus* overtime. Some companies charge one hundred fifty to two hundred dollars an hour for overtime! One bride and groom in this situation wound up paying the limo company two hundred dollars in extra fees. It's much smarter to keep the limo driver on call so that you can call his office to dispatch him when he's needed. Ask about time arrangements and extra fees.

∼ Get a contract written up with all the details of your agreement, including the number of cars you'll need, where and when each of them is to report, deposits, and the signature or name of the person who took your reservation. Again, this is a larger expense, so you'll want to protect your investment. Plus, if one of the three limousines you've hired to transport the bridal party doesn't show up, you have proof that you're entitled to a partial refund.

∼ If friends or relatives have special connections at a limousine company, ask if they might be able to get you a discount. Perhaps they could consider it their wedding present to you.

Limousines aren't the only way to travel. Look into other forms of transportation.

∼ Book a luxury sedan rather than a limousine. These cars are just as sleek and special, some with tinted windows for a little privacy. Be sure to ask for the newest model and contract for the car to be washed and waxed right before your big day.

One couple tried to save by hiring a sedan, which showed up dirty and covered with salt from its previous long rides on winter roads.

∼ Compare prices at car rental agencies—especially those that offer luxury or exotic cars. It might be cheaper to rent a convertible or even an Excalibur for an hour (to the ceremony and reception only), rather than a limo.

∼ Check out classic and antique car associations for prices and availability. In most cases you can make your getaway in a classic that says more about your personalities than a standard limo, and the prices are often much less expensive.

∼ Look in the Yellow Pages or in bridal magazines for special transportation such as horse-and-carriage rides. Research these carefully and always go to see the horse and carriage. Consider here, though, the traffic in your area. Will this horse and carriage have to cross a four-lane highway to get to the reception?

∼ Enlist the help of a friend with a nice car, possibly a convertible. With this free option, you're more likely to be able to decorate this car with streamers and "Just Married" signs than you are with a rented car or limousine.

 If you live close to the ceremony and the reception, consider a walking procession from place to place. On a comfortable day, your parade will be great fun for everyone and the center of attention. Older or disabled guests can be driven the short distance, of course.

 Have your parents or honor attendants drive you to and from the airport for your honeymoon. It's much smarter than hiring a limo, you don't have to worry about a waiting limousine driver and a ticking clock, and you get a better welcome home.

For the Bridal Party

 Of course, limousines for the bridal party aren't a necessity, but if you wish to provide them you should comparison shop among limousine companies. Since you'll be renting more than one limo, try for a group rate.

 Figure out how many limousines you'll need before you start shopping. One is for you and the groom, obviously. Depending on how many bridesmaids and ushers are in your bridal party, you'll have to order more limousines.

∼ Don't attempt to cram ten people into one limousine. Remember the women's dresses shouldn't be crushed and wrinkled by overcrowding in a car. Consider adequate space while tallying cars.

∼ Have helpful relatives and friends drive the bridal party around in their nice cars—cleaned, of course. Convertibles are fun for the celebrating group, so offer your car as well if you have one.

∼ If you have a large bridal party, don't book four or five limos to haul them around on the wedding day. Rent a party bus from the limo company instead. It often turns out to be much less expensive, and most bridal parties report that they love the atmosphere. Some party buses come equipped with great sound systems, mood lighting, comfortable chairs, and—perhaps most important after a long night of partying—a working rest room.

∼ The hotel your guests are staying at may provide free shuttle service. Most hotels have their own fleet of minibuses or vans to take their guests to and from airports and major shopping centers, so ask if you can schedule the bus to take your guests to the ceremony, reception, and back afterward. If you've booked a significant block of rooms for your guests, or if you're holding your reception at that hotel's ballroom, the event manager may allow you to use the shuttle for free or for a low fee.

~ The bridal party can drive themselves in a decorated minivan if one is available to them. Your parents', perhaps? Randi was able to arrange minivan transportation for her bridal party. Not only was it a "party bus," as she called it, but it didn't cost her a dime. The van was her parents'.

~ After the reception, the bridal party may either be dropped off by a designated driver in his or her car, or if there will be no drinking, they can drive themselves home. A smart move would be to have the bridal party drop their cars off in the reception hall parking lot before the ceremony.

For the Guests

~ Before the wedding day, have the bridal party, friends, and relatives help transport out-of-town guests from the airport into town or to your house. No need to hire a shuttle or transport for them; this could cost you fifty to one hundred dollars depending on the number of guests coming in. You could pick them up yourself, but you might be too busy with final plans and fittings.

~ If many guests will be coming into town from far away, consider renting (or borrowing) a minivan to take them from the hotel to the ceremony, to the reception, then back to the hotel at the end of the evening. This mass transit may be less expensive than driving everyone in separate cars. Again, the hotel may have a free shuttle for their use around town.

24

Music for the Ceremony

The right music can add a lovely element to any wedding ceremony. This chapter shares ideas on how to hire musicians for less, get performances for free, and add a priceless personal touch to your day.

∼ First, check with the wedding officiant about your plans for music during the ceremony. You don't want to hire a harpist for one hundred fifty dollars and then find out that the church does not allow outside performers or the secular music you've selected. Another reason to talk to the officiant: he or she may have several weddings to perform that day—all within tight time constraints—and your music may put your ceremony time over the limit. Unfair, I know. But it does happen. It's best to ask first.

 ∼ Have as one of your criteria for choosing a wedding site the free service of the location's choir.

 ∼ Remember, though, that the organist isn't always free. Tipping him or her is usually required.

 ∼ If a relative, friend, or bridal party member is a professional musician, such as a harpist, pianist, or flutist, ask that person to perform at the ceremony as a wedding gift to you.

 ∼ Ask your local high school or college choir to perform for a small fee, usually a donation to their upcoming trips and supplies fund. Some schools have specialty performing groups, such as madrigal choirs and even string quartets, as well.

 ∼ Place an ad in a college newspaper for a harpist or flutist to perform at your wedding. No doubt you'll soon be flooded with calls from talented young people searching for experience, résumé material, and a payment far below those expected by professional musicians. Anne paid just twenty-five dollars for the harpist who performed at her wedding. It was the young harpist's first job, and Anne loved her music. A professional she called while researching musicians claimed a two-hundred-dollar fee. Just be sure to first listen to the performer you hire.

~ Rather than hiring a soloist, why don't you sing a song to the groom yourself? Or have him sing to you. (This only works if you have a bit more singing experience than just performing "My Girl" on the karaoke machine.)

~ If your wedding will be held outdoors, have some of your wedding music played over a good stereo sound system. You can get a tape of classical or designated wedding music for free in the library.

~ When choosing music to be played at your wedding, consider adding a wedding song from your heritage. Either give your choice of sheet music to the performer you've chosen, or once again get a cassette of that music free in your public library.

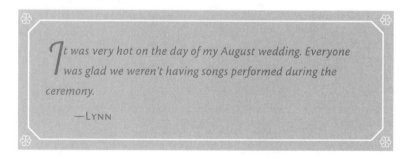

It was very hot on the day of my August wedding. Everyone was glad we weren't having songs performed during the ceremony.

—LYNN

Or, for the biggest savings and not too large an effect on your ceremony, you could choose not to have a pianist, harpist, flutist, or choir perform a song during or before your wedding. The church organist, perhaps, could be allowed to play the processional, a hymn, and the recessional. It might be a bit boring, but it is traditional. Actually, not too many people will expect more than the standard organist, so you're off the hook if this is your choice.

25

The Photographer and Videographer

With the average photography package costing three thousand dollars and the average videography package costing one thousand three hundred dollars, you're looking at a large expense for what is arguably a very important part of the day. You're paying for a permanent record of your wedding day, which adds up to a large amount for the finished products. Couples who try to save money often make a big mistake in underspending, and they pay the price later when they wind up with too few photos and a grainy wedding video. Learn how to find the happy middle ground of securing the best photos and footage for far less than average prices.

The Photographer

∾ When hiring a professional photographer, it's very important to comparison shop. Not only are you looking for the best prices and the best packages, you're also looking at the photographers' samples and the quality of their work. Are they dependable? Do they offer extras? Keep track of each photography service you consider so that you may narrow down the field later and choose from the best.

∾ Ask a recently married friend to recommend her photographer. If she raves about his or her work and has attractive albums and portraits to support the glowing review, your search for quality has landed on a target. If the price is right, this photographer is a good choice.

∾ Note that membership in the Professional Photographer's Association of America means the photographer is well trained. It's a good way to check credentials.

∾ Hire a photographer who has at least five years of experience shooting weddings. A well-trained photographer can place all of your shots better, can assemble and capture group shots in less time than an amateur, and will get you better pictures than someone with little wedding experience. Hiring a true professional, especially given that expense, is the best investment.

$\sim$ When looking through photographers' sample albums and photographs, look not only for focus and a pretty subject (they'll of course show you only their best work) but also for pictures taken in different lighting and different settings, a variation of vertical and horizontal shots, more candid than stiff posed shots, special lenses, and whatever other ideas you have for your album. You'll want to be sure you're getting every penny's worth when you hand over what could be a pretty hefty check.

$\sim$ A quick check with the Better Business Bureau can reveal if any of your final choices for photographer have had any charges or complaints against them. You should know of your photographer's and videographer's past records if you're to trust them with such an important event.

$\sim$ A less costly option would be to hire the photographer only for the ceremony and the beginning of your reception. After all, these are the most important times to capture. Plus, everyone looks their best the first half of the celebration. After a few hours guests look tired, makeup fades, and hairstyles fall. There would be no need to keep the photographer for the full five hours of the reception . . . particularly if your guests have cameras of their own. You can always get prints of their candid dancing scenes. One bride saved five hundred dollars with this option, and she noticed no difference in the quality of the photos from her reception.

~ In your paying for the photographer's (and videographer's) time on your wedding day, every minute spent from the time of his arrival to his departure is on the clock. Keep that in mind when scheduling any break time between the ceremony and reception. Some brides schedule an hour or two-hour break before the reception starts, which is wasted money if the photographer is just standing around waiting for the next phase of the wedding to start.

~ Go through the photographers' lists of available packages. What is the minimum number of pictures you will need? Do you really need one thousand regular prints, twelve eight-by-tens, thirty four-by-fives, and one hundred wallets? You can save a lot of money by ordering just the number of pictures you'll need—to keep for yourself and to give as gifts.

TIP FROM THE PROS

Dennis Tessler of The Pros, a national wedding services company, gives the following advice: "The average wedding photographer takes between two hundred and three hundred pictures, which is way more than you need. A total of one hundred fifty to two hundred pictures gives you a great variety without having to pay for so many extra shots to be developed. You'd rather have one out of three photos to choose from for a forty-eight-page album than one out of every five. Having a great, well-trained photographer maximize the value of the film and developing is going to save you money. Don't go lower than one hundred fifty to two hundred pictures, though. Your wedding photos are an important documentation of your day, and you'll want to have a better selection."

~ Don't be bullied by a set price package. See if you can pick and choose the photos you really want (you may not need wallet-sized photos) and negotiate the price accordingly. It's in the package that the photographers rake in the cash, so assemble your package well.

⌒ If the photographer's package offers you the full set of proofs to keep for free, you're getting a nice stack of pictures that you would have had to pay for otherwise.

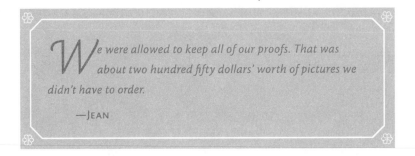

We were allowed to keep all of our proofs. That was about two hundred fifty dollars' worth of pictures we didn't have to order.

—JEAN

⌒ Ask for your proofs to be delivered on disk or on contact sheets rather than as regular photos. This eliminates the cost of delivering all of the proofs and you still can get a good look at the photos you have to choose from.

⌒ The best photography companies will give you the negatives of your wedding photos once the pictures are developed. In the photography industry, companies make their money off the back end, charging a fortune for reprints, enlargements, and other new orders over time. Dennis Tessler of The Pros says that these reprint charges can be fifteen to twenty times the cost of production, so you'd be best served to get the negatives and find a less expensive developer. A warning, though:

you won't find too many companies that will give you negatives for free, but you can negotiate to buy negatives for larger savings in the long run.

~ Choose your album carefully. At the average photography studio it can cost more than one hundred fifty dollars just for the album alone, without pictures! Choose a plain album, skipping the leather and decorated styles, as the real beauty will be inside the album. Don't pay to have your names printed on the album, as that's an extra cost as well.

~ Create a smaller formal bridal album. Go for a twenty-four- or thirty-six-page album rather than a forty-eight-page one. You'll still have your wedding pictures from the proofs you choose, or get to keep for free, plus the candids taken at the wedding by guests' cameras. The larger portrait-style photos in your main album are great for display, but you don't need many if you're on a budget.

~ If you don't want to decrease the number of pages in your album, you can certainly choose to have fewer shots in the parents' albums without them noticing the difference.

~ Don't be pressured into ordering special photo albums from the photographer for parents, grandparents, the bridal party, and others. For half the price of this service you can make your own albums with extra copies of your pictures (perhaps some of the proofs or pictures taken with your camera) and inexpensive store-bought photo albums. You may even do your own wedding album using the professional pictures and a book you've purchased from the store. It all adds up to great savings if you do a good enough job arranging the pictures in the albums.

~ It sounds harsh, but don't be pressured into ordering special photo albums for people you don't like. Your parents will undoubtedly attempt to push some of their wishes on you throughout the planning of the wedding. This is usually one of them. If Mom wants mean Aunt Bertha to have some pictures, let Mom pay for it.

~ Another money-saving approach to the photographer's package is to order a percentage of your pictures in black and white. It may be cheaper, depending on your photographer, and these shots look very elegant. Besides, these pictures will not fade as quickly as color prints will. Check price comparisons carefully.

~ Some brides choose to skip the professional bridal portrait, usually taken several weeks before the wedding.

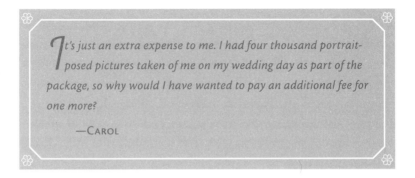

It's just an extra expense to me. I had four thousand portrait-posed pictures taken of me on my wedding day as part of the package, so why would I have wanted to pay an additional fee for one more?

—CAROL

~ Skip the gimmick shots. Do you really need to pay extra for a picture of the two of you superimposed over the sheet music of "your song"? While it might be a fun memento, it's also a nonessential.

~ Skip the expensive editing fees and extras such as cropping photos, adding borders, retouching, matting, and the like.

~ Get a copy of the contract, just to clarify the specifics of your agreement and the package you've chosen, and keep your payment receipts in case any questions arise.

~ While many brides consider the wedding pictures too important to be left to an amateur, you may weigh your options differently. A friend or relative with plenty of photography experience can do just as wonderful a job as a pro, and he or she has the added advantage of knowing your guests and know-ing what pictures you'll really want. Plus, you won't be charged anywhere near the fee of a professional photographer. If your friend will lend his or her picture-snapping services for free as a wedding gift to you, you should supply him or her with more than enough film to last through the ceremony, reception, and post-reception events. But don't look for cheap film to cut costs here. You want to get the best film you can. Just remember how much you're already saving by not hiring a photographer. Of course you'll pay for developing the film yourself, so keep this in mind when you buy your film—consider how many pictures you'll really need, then buy accordingly.

~ Have two friends take pictures at the ceremony. Both could work the ceremony, providing different perspectives, and they could then take turns capturing special moments of the reception.

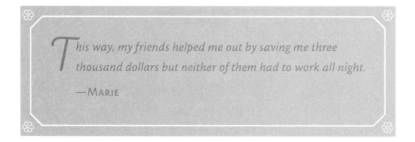

This way, my friends helped me out by saving me three thousand dollars but neither of them had to work all night.

—MARIE

∽ Buy multipacks or cases of high-quality film such as Kodak at bulk discount stores like Costco and Sam's Club.

∽ Buy film with more exposures per roll. This usually is the most economical way to go, although you should always check prices.

∽ Have your volunteers use their cameras so they don't have to learn the intricacies of someone else's during the ceremony. This is no time for trial and error. If, however, you have an outstanding camera and would prefer to use it for the wedding photos, give the camera to your volunteer a week or two before the wedding with a roll or two of film—just so he or she can get the hang of using it. Saving money usually means taking extra care to prevent the worst from happening.

CAMERA RESOURCES

Best Camera—888-237-8226

Boecks Camera—800-700-5090

EPP Wedding Products—412-823-6748

 Tell your friend to take several shots of the major parts of the ceremony and reception so you won't lose all record of your first kiss if the one picture of it didn't come out. Several shots will be your insurance.

 Many brides are choosing to put one of those throwaway cameras on each table at the reception. Guests then take candid shots of you, themselves, and all the dancing and fun going on around you. While you're dancing your first dance, Cousin Fred may be taking his cue to propose to his girlfriend . . . finally. Moments like these don't have to get away. Just make sure you don't overspend on those throwaway cameras. Each one will cost you anywhere from eight to fifteen dollars, depending on where you shop—plus developing. If you figure the costs wisely, you can still do this and cut your wedding picture spending.

 When comparison shopping for picture developing, consider that on-site developing may turn out to be less expensive than mail-order developing. Investigate the numbers.

 Keep in mind that development problems are far more likely to occur at photo shops than with a professional photographer's lab. If you do choose to go this route, be sure to choose a photo-developing shop that has up-to-date equipment and a well-trained developing expert.

~ Do not go to one of those one-hour developing places just because you can't wait to see your wedding photos. You'll just wind up paying three to five times extra for the convenience. Save some money and wait those few days.

~ If you'll be turning in fifty rolls of film, see if you can negotiate for a lower, bulk developing price. You may get 5 or 10 percent off. It adds up.

The Videographer

~ You may think that the wedding video is a rather unimportant part of the day. After all, you're going to be there and it's the memories in your head that will last forever. While video pros warn against cutting expenses by eliminating the wedding video—or by asking a family member to take the footage—remember that your video is going to be more important to you ten years later than it is the week after your wedding. Not only is it a recording of your vows, your first dance, your cutting of the cake, it's a living memory of your loved ones. Over time, people age or pass away. In your video you'll have priceless footage of your uncle Augie laughing and singing with his brothers and sisters. You'll have footage of your father looking proudly at you. In the years to come, when these people are no longer in your life, you'll have this tape to remember them during the happiest times of their lives. I say often that it's a mistake to cut too deeply into your budget just to save money. The wedding video, for this reason, is worth some extra expense.

〜 Ask a friend to recommend her videographer, then take a look at her wedding video to see if it's the sort you would like. This is the best way to be sure you're getting your money's worth.

〜 Comparison shop, again not only for price but for packages and quality. Look at the videographer's samples—the full-length ones, not the snippets of his or her best work. Look for focus, good lens work, graphics, smooth transitions, and soundtrack clarity.

〜 Talk to the videographer about her equipment. Much has been written in bridal articles about having professionals use two- or three-chip cameras for a better product. Dennis Tessler of The Pros says that three-chip cameras are fine if you're shooting for television or the movies, but a regular VHS camera will do the job extremely well for weddings. Digital cameras are all the rage now, but experts say that this form of technology is still young, not yet tested over time, and may even produce a tape that fades in years to come. The new DVD options are not standardized yet, either. "There are many different formats in DVD. What works in some machines may not work in others," says Tessler. Stick with VHS cameras for capturing your big day. "VHS will still be around five to eight years from now. Later on, the footage can be transferred to DVD."

∼ A true professional can do an in-camera edit, choosing shots well so that there is less need for heavy editing later on. Talk to your video pro about this practice. Cutting down on editing time will save you money later on.

∼ You can save several hundred dollars by forgoing the post-shooting edit. Videographer Steve Blahitka of Back East Productions in East Hanover, New Jersey, suggests buying the raw footage of your wedding for great savings. This is how it works: your professional videographer uses his experience to get the great shots, in-camera edits, and then simply hands you the tape at the end of the night. No costly, by-the-hour editing fee means big savings and you get to see your tape far sooner.

∼ Ask the videographer about his or her style. You don't want the video camera in your face all night, so make sure the videographer can get the footage without being underfoot. And ask what he or she wears to weddings. A suit? Tuxedo? Make sure this person will dress appropriately—this is your wedding.

~ Leave out special effects. This isn't Hollywood. It's your wedding video and you don't need all the fancy editing work and effects that wind up dating your tape and distracting from the images. In addition, some effects are copyrighted, such as Disney characters, and cannot be used by the public.

~ Choose your video package carefully. How much time do you really think you'll need? Do you want to spend money on film of you getting ready in the morning? How many copies do you really need?

~ Skip the option of having two cameras set in different places during the wedding. Some videographers say that you'll get a more finished final product, with better angles and more big moments captured, but what you're doing is paying for double the manpower and double the editing time. Choose the single-camera option. A good professional will not miss any important shots.

~ As with everything having to do with your planning, get a copy of your contract as a record of your agreement, complete with specific details and the videographer's signature or name. Keep all receipts as proof of payment.

〜 While most experts agree that professional videography is the best investment, you may not have enough in your budget to warrant the use of a pro or may not have a large emotional investment in a top-notch video. In these cases, you can ask a reliable friend or relative to help out as a gift to you. Just realize that the quality will be lessened, as an amateur doesn't have the focus or devotion a professional would have.

〜 Have two or three friends tape your wedding and reception with their video cameras from different angles. A good editing job will give your tape a professional look.

COMPARE AND SAVE

Professional videographer .... $1,200–$2,000
Friends helping out .... free

〜 Of course, you'll supply the videotapes for your volunteer videographers. Again, don't buy cheap tapes—the quality of the picture and sound will reflect the price you paid. Instead, spend the money for quality equipment.

~ Don't buy too many tapes. Look instead for long-running tapes and allow yourself several. Before shopping, figure out the amount of time the tapes will have to cover and get a bit more than that. If the amount of time warrants it, arrange to buy your tapes in bulk.

~ If your videographer will be using your video camera, give it to him or her a few days before the wedding to get used to it and its functions. Teach your friend how to use it. Point out fade-in, scanning, zooming, speed of movement, and so on. Then view together the practice filming.

~ Discuss where the videographers will be set up during the ceremony and reception. It's a good idea to bring these volunteers to the rehearsal so that they can map out their positioning and instructions, as well as to note any restrictions for your wedding location.

~ Set up a system whereby your volunteer videographer can easily keep track of which tapes are used and unused throughout the wedding day—perhaps with stickers or different cases for full tapes. You don't want a confused camera operator to record over your vows to get the throwing of the garter.

∽ When you have the tapes, arrange your editing. Either do it yourself or ask a talented friend to help. Professional videographers aren't the only ones who can create an introduction filled with your old baby pictures and stills of the two of you during your dating years.

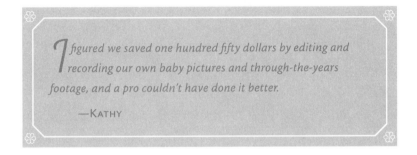

I figured we saved one hundred fifty dollars by editing and recording our own baby pictures and through-the-years footage, and a pro couldn't have done it better.

—KATHY

∽ If you're planning to make copies of your wedding video for family and friends, copy your master tape onto a quality videotape, and then use that copy to make all the other copies. You don't want to put too much strain on your master tape. After all, you'll be viewing it yourself many times.

After the wedding, thank your friends and relatives who acted as photographers and videographers with nice gifts and notes of your gratitude. Their kindness and willingness to help has not only saved you a great deal of money, but they've also given you a priceless gift you'll undoubtedly cherish forever.

26

Wedding Programs

The program for your wedding day lets your guests know what to look forward to during your ceremony and who its participants are. Most important, the program remains one of your cherished keepsakes after the wedding. You can create beautiful programs for far less than standard commercial prices with the advice in this chapter.

⌒ Instead of ordering plain programs from the bridal stationery store or catalog—usually the same place you've ordered your invitations from—make your own. With a quality computer, your options are endless, and you have creative control over the process. Plus, today's paper companies are creating beautiful bridal-themed program paper at a cost of under ten dollars for a pack of twenty-four. Some designs match the printer-ready styles of place cards and thank-you cards. See Chapter 19 for resources.

COMPARE AND SAVE

Store-bought programs .... $75–$125

Homemade programs .... $15–$40

~ Look first at examples of wedding programs, either the ones from your cousins' weddings or those featured in bridal magazines. Aside from their format, what special additions would you like for your own?

~ Draw up your program, with precise wording and an idea of your layout. You'll need to know how many pages your program will be to figure copying costs. Of course, if you can fit your program on four sides (the fronts and backs of each side of a folded paper) you'll only need one sheet of paper for each program.

~ If you like the look of calligraphy but don't trust your hand at it, use the calligraphy font on your home computer. You'll get flawless letters along with a neat page setup and (depending on your program) the ability to view the page on the screen without having to print it out first. There's no better way to save money on a professional-looking, personal job.

~ Save even more money by printing your programs on your computer. Use quality white paper or parchment bought by the pound or in bulk at any discount or stationery store.

~ If your printer isn't top quality and your ink and paper are expensive, see if you can beat those costs by taking your master copy to a discount printer. Depending on the paper you choose, the total cost may be less, and the results look great.

~ A decorative cover for your program is always a nice touch. Look in stationery stores and religious bookstores to find a good selection of program covers, and comparison shop. They're not very expensive, but you want to get the best price you can.

~ Instead, have an artist friend or relative design and create program covers for you. Again, it could be a gift, and it's a nice personal touch.

COMPARE AND SAVE

Store-bought program covers .... $40–$75

Homemade program covers .... $10–$20

〰 See if your printer will collate your programs and program covers, then bind them at the crease. Many places will do this for free. If not, simply fold each one and slip the program inside the cover unattached.

〰 Unfortunately, as nice as they are, programs may also be seen as nonessentials and cut from the wedding plans. You can live without them.

27

The Guest Book

Among the many items you'll cherish in years to come is your guest book. It's where your guests sign their names and leave you personal messages of good wishes and joy. With the ideas in this chapter you can supply a beautiful guest book without spending the high amounts in certain gift shops and catalogs.

✑ Don't buy one of those fancy, plummy, overpriced guest registry books in the bridal salon or in a bridal supply catalog. Instead, get a plain one at a discount stationery store. A white cover that says nothing is every bit as classy and appropriate as the kind with the shiny gold lettering and picture.

✑ A wedding guest book is a great gift idea from the flower girl and ring bearer or other member of the wedding party.

〜 Forget the frilly feather pen that usually comes with those bridal guest book sets. A plain gold or white one you already own will do just as well.

〜 Make your own personalized guest book from a plain, unused journal, or designate the back pages of your personal wedding journal for the signatures and messages of your guests.

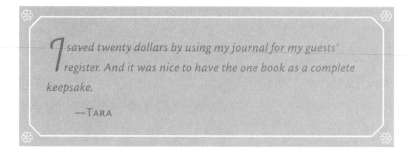

I saved twenty dollars by using my journal for my guests' register. And it was nice to have the one book as a complete keepsake.

—TARA

〜 Appoint someone to be in charge of taking the guest book to the ceremony location, to the reception, and back home afterward. You don't want the book to be misplaced.

28

Decorating the Reception Location

You've seen advertisements and pictures of lavishly decorated ballrooms and banquet halls. Enormous floral centerpieces crown every table, ice sculptures highlight the buffet table, and billowing drapes of fabric with twinkling white lights hung from the ceiling transform the room into a magical scene. But what you don't see is the bill for such accoutrements. Decor is big business and those lofty images demand a big investment. But you're not doomed to crepe-paper streamers and white balloons if your budget doesn't allow for the grand scenario. You can incorporate expensive looks for a lot less, choose equally impressive alternative decor ideas, and use your talents to design a million-dollar look for a fraction of the cost. Your guests won't be able to tell the difference.

◡ For an informal wedding, plain balloons are less expensive than the shiny, Mylar ones, and bunches of these are every bit as festive as the fancier selections.

◡ White balloons may be less expensive than colored ones, depending on where you're shopping.

◡ Borrow an air compressor to blow up the balloons, or rent a helium tank and buy balloons on sale at a party store. Shop around for the best buys.

◡ Use strings of white Christmas lights you already own to adorn trees or the ceiling in a dimly lit room.

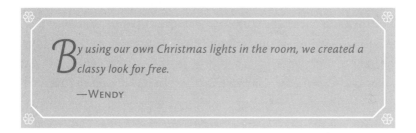

By using our own Christmas lights in the room, we created a classy look for free.

—WENDY

◡ Borrow white or colored Christmas lights from your family and friends to decorate a larger or outdoor setting for next to nothing.

∼ Decorate the walls and buffet table with silver-framed pictures of you and your fiancé, your parents and siblings at their weddings, your fiancé's relatives at their weddings. This is a favorite of many brides today. It's a touching tribute to special relatives, and it's virtually free.

∼ Decorate a ceiling or gazebo roof with mobiles you can make yourself. Choose from hearts, sparkles, crystals, stars, whatever you'd like. If you question the idea of mobiles, just hang straight lines with decorations at the ends. The result is your own starry sky.

∼ Commission an artist or a culinary institute student to make an ice sculpture for you. Put an ad on the bulletin boards at a nearby school announcing your need for a sculptor. You may be able to have a sculpture made for around eighty dollars or even less, depending on its size and complexity.

∼ Rather than renting a trellis, use the one that's already in your yard or at the reception location.

∼ Check out theme party books in your local library to find ideas for your theme wedding. You don't need a party planner for this.

∼ For a theme wedding, use the items you have handy. For example, if you're planning a Mexican fiesta wedding, use your brother's souvenir sombrero as one of the decorations. Use your patterned rugs and throws as well. If you rented these items and others like them, you'd pay up to one hundred fifty dollars easily.

∼ If you don't own it, see if you can borrow it. If you can't borrow it, see if you can make it. If you can't make it, rent it.

∼ At the very least, play up the natural attractions of the reception location. If there's a lovely view of the sunset, for example, part of the atmosphere is already set. Minimal decor is needed otherwise. So try to see your location at the time of day when your party will be taking place so you can get a look at the natural lighting and features.

29

Planning the Menu

Most often it's the food that guests remember. If the food is good, you'll hear raves. If it's not, you'll hear complaints. Many couples try too hard to save in this area of the expenses, but this is one place where you can't cut the budget too much. You get what you pay for. You can create a delicious, unique, and impressive menu by following the cost-saving tips in this chapter. Caterers and chefs alike tell me that they can answer to any budget challenge and still provide top-quality menu items that you and your guests will savor.

∼ Before you can contract a caterer, you'll need to know exactly what kind of reception you'll be having—level of formality, theme, location, time of day. As mentioned previously, an earlier wedding is a less formal one and is therefore less expensive because you will not be serving a full sit-down dinner. An afternoon wedding means you'll most likely be serving hors d'oeuvres and cake and coffee. An early evening wedding, before 8:00 P.M., usually includes a full dinner or buffet, and an after-8 reception is often served by hors d'oeuvres and cake again. So obviously you'll need to know what kind of package and menu you're looking for before you can settle on a caterer.

〜 Do your research to compare the caterers available to you. Compare general costs, of course, along with other package elements such as equipment, linens, cleanup, and the like. Keep track of your notes and comparisons so that you can narrow the choices down when you're ready to make your final decision.

〜 Ask a recently married friend or relative to recommend the caterer who did her reception. If you remember the food at her reception as particularly outstanding and the service as exemplary, then you'll be able to make your choice based on experience. Several brides report savings of 10 to 15 percent as referrals from previous customers. Caterers depend on word-of-mouth advertisement, and you could save.

〜 When you're researching caterers, do the introductory work over the phone, but always go to the business in person for the next step. You'll want to see their samples, their linens and china if that's part of the package, and their overall appearance as a successful business. While there, see if you can arrange to taste their menu selections. Many caterers expect this request as part of today's smart wedding shopping, and they keep a supply of hors d'oeuvres on hand.

~ Ask for references, then use them. Place a call to several of their recent clients and—knowing that, of course, only people who were happy with the caterer's work will be referred to you—ask about the good qualities of the caterer's service.

~ A good standard by which to measure possible caterers is their membership in the International Food Service Executive Association. Membership in this organization listed on the company's business card means the caterer is well trained and has met the requirements of the association.

~ The Better Business Bureau can tell you if any charges or complaints have been registered against the caterers you're researching. A good history in the business is a positive indication of their reliability, whereas a negative mark could make you think twice about investing in that business's services. After all, it's your wedding.

~ Use your best instincts when researching caterers. Are they forthcoming with information? Do they seem willing to go by your wishes, or do they seem to want to be in control? Do they seem organized? Do you feel comfortable with them?

When you've settled on a caterer, choose your menu carefully. The courses and foods you choose will undoubtedly affect the price you're paying, so follow these hints from brides who have been there.

~ Choose a menu that is right for the season of your wedding. Some heavier foods should not be served in the summer.

~ Ask for a price list for each type of entrée or appetizer. Your caterer should be able to provide you with this information so you can tell at a glance which choices are less expensive.

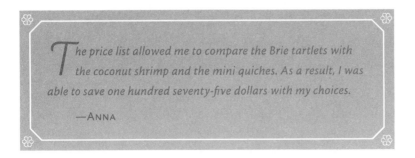

The price list allowed me to compare the Brie tartlets with the coconut shrimp and the mini quiches. As a result, I was able to save one hundred seventy-five dollars with my choices.

—ANNA

~ Choose more popular, simpler foods. Exotic choices mean more money. Chef Jerome Louie of the Bernards Inn in Bernardsville, New Jersey, suggests asking your caterer about his or her creative choices in chicken and pasta dishes.

～ Choose a less expensive option of a pricey dish. For instance, choose medallions of beef or beef tenderloin rather than filet mignon. A great chef can prepare these options with flair and taste, plus great presentation, and your guests will never know that you saved ten dollars per plate with this choice.

～ Look into prices for combination dinners. Chef Jerome Louie suggests an entrée featuring two grilled jumbo shrimp and several medallions of beef. Combination plates can cost less, depending on your selections, and they give your guests a better variety of food.

～ Try something beyond the usual bridal menu fare. For instance, instead of filet mignon, chicken marsala, and salmon, consider Australian rack of lamb. Unique choices may be priced lower.

～ Select more inexpensive food stations for the cocktail hour. There is no need for a carved meat station during the pre-party when you're paying for a meat entrée during the dinner. Chef Jerome Louie suggests creative pasta and vegetable stations, in-season seafood stations, and passed hors d'oeuvres.

～ Skip the big cheese-cube tray during the cocktail hour. It will hardly be touched if you're offering other selections, and it can go bad if left out too long.

~ Don't plan on having a seafood bar or other specialty food bar set up at the reception if other food will be served. While the choice may be appetizing, it's a nonessential. An *expensive* nonessential.

~ Avoid obviously expensive foods such as caviar, filet mignon, and lobster tails.

~ For the entrée, have the caterer offer your guests a choice of a meat or nonmeat entrée. Not only will this lower the price quoted in your contract, you'll please your health-conscious guests.

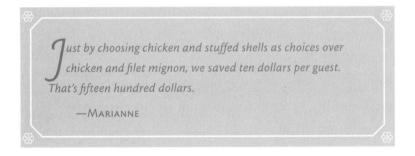

Just by choosing chicken and stuffed shells as choices over chicken and filet mignon, we saved ten dollars per guest. That's fifteen hundred dollars.

—MARIANNE

~ Do you really need several different kinds of vegetables? Cut down the list and save some money. Everyone's going to be saving room for the cake anyway.

∼ Forget the extra dessert trays and the chocolate mousse. Let them eat cake. Savings here could reach thirty dollars per guest.

∼ If you must have other options besides the wedding cake, choose inexpensive but elegant items such as chocolate truffles or chocolate-dipped strawberries. Talk to your caterer about inexpensive dessert possibilities and select one or two options.

∼ Skip the international coffee bar. Order plain and decaffeinated coffee instead.

∼ The manner in which the food is served may also affect the caterer's final bill. Rather than set out a big tray of shrimp cocktail or other appetizers, caterers strongly recommend having these items passed butter-style by servers. This way each guest's portion is controlled and the caterer's fees for these menu choices are lowered.

∼ Or arrange a more economical deal with your caterer. Have them prepare the food, and you do the rest. You pick it up, set it up, and clean it up.

∼ Or along the same lines, contract for only half of the meal to be catered. The caterer does the entrée, and you do the appetizers and desserts.

~ Don't go for expensive food decorations and displays. You don't need a shrimp cocktail sculpture in the shape of a three-dimensional heart, do you? Believe it or not, you could wind up paying up to three hundred dollars for a food sculpture such as this.

~ Arrange for some members of your bridal party and perhaps some relatives and friends to help out in the kitchen a few days before the wedding.

~ Get a copy of the contract, including a full, in-detail listing of the package and menu you're purchasing from them. As an added precaution, get the name of the person who took your order, and write down the date and time it was taken. Keep all payment receipts and perhaps even a copy of your check, in case of conflict over the bill later on.

> *The caterer swore that I had one more payment to make, when I was sure I had already paid it in cash. Basically, she won, and I had to pay her another two hundred fifty dollars.*
>
> —BONNIE

If you'll be catering the reception yourself, consider the following tips.

~ Use the menus you've found in the caterers' brochures to plan your appetizers and entrées. You'll find you can plan and serve identical meals for a fraction of caterers' prices.

~ Plan your menu around popular, inexpensive foods such as pasta, chicken, and in-season seafoods.

~ Use your favorite recipes. This is no time to try new ones.

~ If you'd like to serve some ethnic foods at your reception, check with your local heritage organization. They may be able to help you with recipes, pricing, and even their own frozen selections. One bride received a big 30 percent discount and some help in the kitchen from her heritage association's expert cooks.

~ Borrow the extra equipment you'll need, such as baking pans, stockpots, and so on. No need to rent them.

~ Shop in bulk. Check wholesale markets for the ingredients you'll need.

∼ Make use of your warehouse club membership, or go as a guest on a friend's membership.

∼ When pricing food and supplies, always shop by unit prices. You can always discover hidden bargains that way.

∼ Buy foods that are in season—they're less expensive.

∼ Always try a new recipe months in advance so you don't find out too late that it doesn't work or tastes terrible.

∼ Plan to buy trays of specialty food from your local deli or the takeout section at the caterer's. Just transfer the Swedish meatballs and bacon-wrapped Brie onto serving plates, and you have catered quality for a near homemade price.

∼ Garnish plates of your appetizers to give them a professional look. Your guests will never know.

∼ Decorate the appetizer table with flowers and framed pictures so that the full table makes it look like there's more food.

∼ Volunteer helpers can set up, serve, and clean up. Good people to ask are friends of your younger brother (he'll have a better time if they're there) and your friends' children.

30

Beverages

There will be many toasts and trips to the bar for your guests, so you'll want to find the most economical way to supply drinks. Don't cut expenses too deeply here, as you won't want your guests to toast you with something you wouldn't drink on a bet. Forget about a cash bar; that's an insult and a major no-no in the wedding world today. Here you'll learn how to arrange top-notch beverages for your guests at a bargain, without the savings showing.

◇ For some brides, the idea of an open bar goes without saying. Their families would expect no less, and they'd consider a cash bar to be an attack on their station in life. So instead of canceling the open bar and risking the wrath of your relatives, choose instead to limit the choices offered at that open bar. Have the bartender offer a smaller range of wines, mixed drinks, and soft drinks instead of opening the place's full stock to your guests.

~ Choose to serve nonalcoholic drinks only. Punch stretches a long way. (*Or* add some champagne for taste and fizz.)

~ Close the bar early. Not only will you save money, but your guests will have more time to dance off their champagne before having to leave.

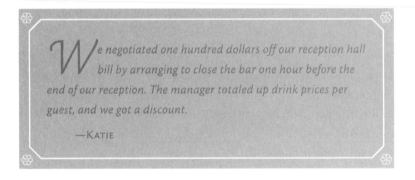

We negotiated one hundred dollars off our reception hall bill by arranging to close the bar one hour before the end of our reception. The manager totaled up drink prices per guest, and we got a discount.

—Katie

~ Provide your own alcohol and drink mixes rather than go by the reception hall's prices. Surely you can find a less expensive wine. Be aware of whether the establishment charges a corkage fee, an extra expense when you supply the liquor. It's a big waste of money if you're paying ten dollars each time the bartender opens a bottle of your wine.

~ For information on today's best wines and spirits, plus a reliable price list, check out the highly esteemed Wine Spectator at www.winespectator.com. Here, you'll be able to compare wine information, descriptions of taste, and most important, expense. Be sure to visit your local upscale liquor store to purchase several different bottles a few months beforehand. Invite some friends over for a wine tasting, and make your choices on reds and whites for your reception. Two months or so before your wedding, consult with the liquor store manager for a discount on several cases of the chosen vintages.

~ Check first to see if your location has any liquor restrictions. If you find out too late that it doesn't have a liquor license, you won't be able to use your supplies. That's hundreds of dollars wasted.

~ Tell the bar staff to open wine bottles only as they are needed. This way you can take home any unopened bottles to fill your wine collection. For bigger savings without waste, negotiate for the reception manager to refund you the cost of unused liquor for the night.

~ If your reception location requires you to use their liquor at their prices, negotiate as best you can with the manager. Can you offer only part of their stock to your guests? Can you be reimbursed for unopened bottles?

~ If you're given the choice, arrange to serve only the less expensive brands of beer and wine. Research several months before the wedding to find the best picks and best prices. And do a taste test.

~ Choose punch for the kids instead of soft drinks.

~ You don't have to skip the champagne toast just to save money. Look around for a good domestic champagne, and remember that a cheap bottle of champagne is definitely a cheap bottle of champagne. Sample some choices yourself or ask a friend what she served at her reception.

~ Arrange to provide only one glass of champagne per guest—just for the toast. You'll limit your needs to only eight or ten bottles of champagne, rather than twenty or thirty.

~ Instead of champagne, toast with other drinks. It's the toast itself that counts.

~ Speaking of champagne, you'll need bride and groom toasting flutes. As always, don't just plan on buying the ones in the bridal salon or the bridal catalog. Instead, get pretty plain champagne flutes at a regular department store and tie a satin ribbon around each stem. Or designate the toasting flutes as the maid or matron of honor's wedding gift to you (or the best man's, or the bridal party's, or your best friend's).

⁓ Check with a restaurateur or hotelier friend for extra ice. He or she might let you use the industrial ice machines at little cost.

31

Reception Entertainment

DJ or band? Strolling violinist or a twelve-piece orchestra? Swing dancing or the chicken dance? The entertainers you select will make or break your wedding celebration, so get the most for your money without sacrificing fun and photo opportunities on your big day. The entertainment industry has changed a lot in the past few years, offering new combinations and packages that can help you wow your guests and give everyone a night to remember. Check out this chapter for some smart cost-cutting measures and avoid the deadliest mistake of all: hiring cheap talent.

∼ Consider the type of music you want. The performer you choose should have a broad repertoire, whether classical or pop. A band's inability to play the kind of music you like narrows the field of possibilities by one.

〜 Compare packages. What can each DJ or band offer you? When you compare specifics, you'll get a better idea of what your money will be getting you.

〜 A major factor in choosing the entertainment is the amount of space you'll have available for them. A band works well in a spacious reception hall with a stage, but a wedding at home or in a smaller room creates limitations on your choice. A DJ or soloist is perhaps the better selection for these.

〜 Consider the facilities of your reception location. Level ground is needed for DJs and most bands, and it's best to make sure your location has enough electrical outlets and power. An unforeseen problem means you could lose your entertainment at the last minute, along with the nine hundred dollars you paid for it.

〜 Consider your crowd when searching for a DJ or band. If your guests are older, you'll want to provide music they'll appreciate. The same goes for your younger guests. So arrange music according to what your guests will actually dance to. The type of music will determine the kind of band or DJ you'll get.

〜 If you're having trouble deciding between a DJ or band, treat them as equals when you're comparison shopping and just go for the better prices and packages.

ENTERTAINMENT PACKAGES

A new trend in the wedding entertainment industry is the merging of DJ and band options. You'll see entertainment packages in which you can provide a DJ at your reception, plus a few live performances by a singer or musician. Entertainment professionals are always taking the pulse of what's wanted by brides and grooms, and the rising popularity of this mix-n-match entertainment lineup means that you can practice your negotiating skills once again to book both live and recorded music for your day. According to Dennis Tessler at The Pros (www.prosentertainment.com), you can choose from tiers of entertainment services. On the average, a DJ will cost four hundred to one thousand five hundred dollars for the night. A live band will run three thousand to five thousand dollars. With the mix-n-match system, you can hire one or two DJs, a live singer for three songs, and get an upgraded sound system for one thousand to one thousand five hundred dollars combined. That's getting the best of both worlds for a comparable price. Other options you might find in these new entertainment packages: lighting upgrades and light shows, multiple singers, professional dancers, and party props.

⌁ Not all entertainment companies have caught the wave of the future, and you may find yourself staring at a contract that includes light shows and party props. If these elements are not to your liking, ask to have them removed from the package and the price differential revealed. Remember, wedding professionals are competing among themselves for your business and referrals. You have great negotiating power; use it to get the best service for the best price in this expensive portion of the wedding budget.

～ Compare prices per hour versus flat fees, and figure out how many hours you think your reception will last. Ask your recently married friend how long her reception went on and whether or not she wanted to add on a few more hours at the end of it.

～ Find out what the fees are for adding extra hours at the end of the evening. Your whole group may be having so much fun at the reception that you decide to ask the DJ or band to stay on for one more hour. What are the extra charges for doing so, or is it just another hourly rate? It's important to know this ahead of time, as a decision made at the actual reception could cost you a small fortune in additional fees.

～ Get recommendations from recently married friends, or hire a group you've already seen at another wedding.

〜 Better yet, if you're going to hire a band, go hear them at an actual reception if you can. No one will mind if you step in to listen for a moment.

〜 If you're checking out DJs, find out what he or she will be wearing to the reception. State your preference for a suit or tuxedo for a man, or a dress or tuxedo for a woman.

〜 Specify how many breaks the band will be allowed to take during the reception. You don't want to pay them for five hours of playing when they've really only played for three.

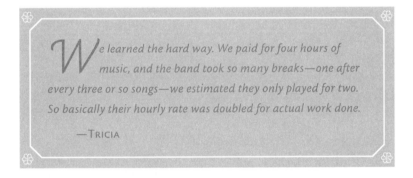

We learned the hard way. We paid for four hours of music, and the band took so many breaks—one after every three or so songs—we estimated they only played for two. So basically their hourly rate was doubled for actual work done.

—Tricia

〜 Draw up a contract, and get signatures for verification. Record the date and time of the contract as well.

〜 As an added precaution—and this comes from a bride who learned a lesson the hard way—specify the kind of music the band will be playing and all of the band members' names.

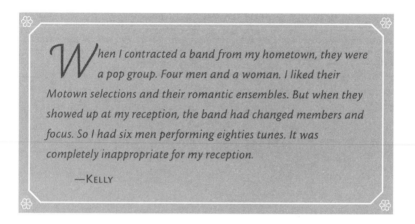

When I contracted a band from my hometown, they were a pop group. Four men and a woman. I liked their Motown selections and their romantic ensembles. But when they showed up at my reception, the band had changed members and focus. So I had six men performing eighties tunes. It was completely inappropriate for my reception.

—KELLY

〜 To avoid the same problem, recognize that bands may change lead singers and selections during the six months between the contract and the wedding. Keep in contact with the band—just tell them you're confirming again—and make sure your contract lets you out of the agreement without monetary obligation if the band should change. (This, by the way, is a reason why DJs are so popular at weddings.)

〜 Give the DJ or band you're hiring a list of songs you'd like to hear at your reception, including special numbers such as line dances and group numbers. Also give them a list of songs you *don't* want them to play. Some songs may remind you of other times, other places, and other people, and you want to make sure they're not a part of your day.

〜 Get a copy of your payment receipt and a copy of your check as proof of payment. Money questions later down the road can be silenced with good record keeping.

〜 If a friend or a family member has a band or is a professional musician, let him or her play for a while, perhaps during the band's breaks. Of course, if your talented acquaintances would like the exposure of working your entire reception— and they sound good to you—arrange an amount you could pay them. If they refuse payment, offer them a free meal instead, or simply accept their performance as a gift. One bride arranged for her stepbrother's band to play at her wedding as his gift to her. The savings: six hundred fifty dollars she would have had to pay to a professional group.

〜 Hire a college or high school musical group to perform at your reception. These young people studying to be professional musicians or instructors take their performances seriously, and you'll only have to pay them a fraction of what you'd pay a professional. If you've arranged for a school group to perform at your ceremony, ask them to work the reception, too. Tell them they can enjoy the party on their breaks.

~ Or ask the person who performed at your ceremony to play a few hours at the reception as well. Using one person for both saves you time and money.

~ Have a friend of the family or a colleague from work act as DJ during your reception. Make sure he or she has experience with this sort of thing, then set up your own sound system and your favorite CDs, and let him or her go to work as a favor or gift to you.

~ Make your own music mixes for this volunteer DJ to play. Alternate fun songs with slow ones, traditional ethnic music with party classics, so that all your favorites are played at your reception.

~ If you're not a good music mixer, get CDs or tapes free from your public library. They'll have a wide range of party tapes, sixties music, and romantic collections for you to borrow.

~ Don't just turn on a CD player in the corner of the room. See if the reception hall has a way of hooking your music up to their hidden sound system.

~ See if your reception hall is able to pipe into the room their own prerecorded classical music.

Dancing to the Music

~ You'll read in the bridal magazines, and friends will make the suggestion, to consider taking professional dancing lessons so that you'll look good on the dance floor. But professional dance lessons, even adult courses given at night at the high school, cost money. Instead, rent a video on ballroom dancing. Learn the basic steps you'll need to get through the spotlight dance and practice together for a while.

~ Enlist the aid of your light-footed parents or grandparents to help you both learn how to do a waltz or the cha-cha. Then, in turn, you can teach them how to do today's line dances. You'll have lots of fun learning together and showing off your new skills at the party.

32

The Cake

The star of the wedding menu is always the cake. Celebrities spend tens of thousands on theirs, knowing that the cake will wind up on a television special or the cover of a magazine. Your cake can be just as beautiful but at a far lower price. Here you'll find out how to select the perfect confection without getting iced on the price.

~ Don't order your cake through a bridal salon. Some offer such services in their bridal packages, but you could wind up paying five hundred dollars for a simple three-tier cake.

~ You'll get a better price if you order your cake from a baker rather than a caterer. Only your comparison shopping can tell you for sure what the specifics are, of course, but this is a general prescript.

~ Use your family's regular bakery. You know they're reliable, you've tasted their cakes before, and you just might get a discount for being a regular customer. One bride recently received a 50 percent discount from her family's regular bakery.

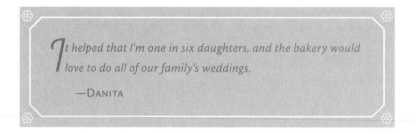

It helped that I'm one in six daughters, and the bakery would love to do all of our family's weddings.

—DANITA

~ Comparison shop at bakeries of different sizes, in different parts of town. Their prices will definitely vary, and you won't always get a better cake in a larger bakery.

~ When comparison shopping at bakeries you've never been to before, always ask to sample a piece of their wedding cakes. It's not as strange a request as it sounds, and it's the best way to be sure you're getting a good cake for your money.

~ Ask a recently married friend where she ordered her wedding cake, and get yours at the same place if the price is right.

〜 If you'll be attending a wedding in the near future, ask the bride where she ordered her cake.

〜 Does the bakery deliver the cake to the reception location for free, or is there a charge? Ask before you order.

〜 When ordering your wedding cake, you'll have to tell the baker how many guests will be in attendance at your wedding. Take ten off your grand total since not everyone eats cake at the reception. There are those who skip the cake because they're dieting, on special medical orders not to have sweets, or too busy dancing to sit down for a slice of cake. The smaller number means you'll be paying that much less for your bakery-made cake. Just don't go too low—you wouldn't want to have guests left without a piece.

〜 At some bakeries, stacked cake layers are less expensive than wedding cake layers that are set up in tiers, separated by decorative columns or swan figurines. Ask your baker about the price difference for a cake with layers stacked instead of supported.

〜 Ask for a copy of the order for your cake, checking twice to make sure the baker has recorded the right size, filling, icing, decorations, date of wedding, location of the reception, and phone number to reach you. A lost or wrong cake is one of the most common wedding blunders, and it's also a waste of your money.

~ Call to confirm the delivery and order of your cake once or twice during the planning months, then once again several days before the wedding.

~ Make sure you choose fillings and frosting that will do well in the weather. A hot summer day could cause your cake to melt right off the table. It has happened. A butter-cream frosting usually holds up better than a frosting made of whipped cream. Keep the cake in the shade and as cool as possible on warm days.

~ Ask for a price list of fillings and cake flavors. It's not all white cake with strawberry filling now, as most bakeries offer such delectable choices as cannoli cream filling, chocolate espresso mousse filling, apricot filling, and more. If you want unique options for your wedding cake, look at a printed price sheet and see what the expenses are. One couple chose a smaller wedding cake so that their guests could feast on rich chocolate cake with cannoli cream filling. The price shift was worth it, as their guests raved about it being the best wedding cake they'd ever had. How's that for a sweet reward?

∼ While the smooth, sculpted look of rolled fondant makes for a great picture and bridal magazine cover shot, it's also far more expensive than traditional frosting with butter-cream icing. At several weddings I've been to there were complaints that although the cake was a work of art, the stiff fondant outer layer was inedible.

∼ Even in the cake industry, time is money. While choosing your cake style and decorations, remember that the intricate design piped in icing on the sides of your cake layers could take hours for a bakery artist to complete. You will pay dearly for it. Yes, it is a beautiful sight when the baker presents a cake that looks like it's covered in lovely Belgian lace, but you'd pay far less for a traditionally frosted cake with piped-on accents or a cascade of fresh flowers. The same price increase applies to marzipan minisculptures that accentuate the cake. The more artistry it takes, the more time it takes, and the more it will cost.

∼ Look through advertisements for a person who makes and decorates wedding cakes as a side job. Ads for this service can be found in regular classified ads or the bridal section of your town newspaper. Investigate and compare prices carefully.

∼ Make the groom's cake yourself.

⌒ Have a relative or friend make the groom's cake.

⌒ Skip the groom's cake altogether, especially if you're having a small or informal wedding.

$\mathcal{O}$n Top of the Cake

You could buy one of those traditional cake-top decorations at the bakery, or you could put something else on the cake.

⌒ Top off your cake with a special item or gift. A crystal heart figurine is a gorgeous topper, but make sure the baker knows exactly how much it weighs and its size so the precious thing doesn't fall off the cake onto the floor. The same goes for anything else you're planning to top your cake with.

⌒ Decorate your cake with flowers. Just wash them well, let them air dry, and make sure they're not poisonous. Check with your baker as to which flowers usually go on cakes as decorations, then check with your florist about the safety of those flowers. Saving money should never be a health hazard.

~ Or see if you can negotiate the cake top for free as part of the cake package.

$\mathcal{T}$he Cake Cutter

~ Don't choose from those offered in bridal salons or bridal catalogs. They're very often not the best buy.

~ Buy a simple silver cake cutter set and decorate the handle with ribbons or silk flowers.

~ Have a young sibling or a special friend give the cake cutter to you as a wedding gift. You may even receive a pretty engraved one.

~ If you're not one to treasure your wedding cake cutter forever, just use the reception hall's serving knife.

~ See if your bakery offers a wedding cake cutter set as part of the wedding cake package.

33

Favors and Mementos

Giving your guests a little something to remember your day is a lovely tradition and way to say "thank you" for sharing in the celebration. With all of the favor options out there, you'll find everything from over-the-top presents that raise eyebrows to embarrassingly cheap-looking items that hit the trash bin right away. Avoid making either mistake by choosing the right favors at the right prices.

Favors

～ The usual sugar-coated almonds wrapped in tulle and ribbons can turn into a costly venture. Shop around for the almonds in different markets—not bridal specialty stores—and look for sales on tulle and ribbon.

~ Homemade chocolate candies packaged in little gift boxes are an economical choice, and you can attach to them the symbolism of the sweetness of marriage. It's not uncommon for brides to make these favors for under twenty-five dollars for all the boxes they'll need.

~ Instead of store-bought sachets, create your own. Just buy potpourri in bulk at a discount store—or make your own following directions in a craft book—and sew it into little packages or wrap it into bundles with squares of tulle. You can always ask a talented friend to help with this job.

~ The wine bottles with the personalized labels are out—which is a good thing, because they are expensive. What's in now are far less expensive packets or decorated boxes of chocolate. You may think that Godiva is automatically out of your budget, but think again. The small ballotins with two chocolate truffles are available for under ten dollars a box at some locations, and nothing says class like the gold-wrapped Godiva box. It's the Tiffany of chocolates, and your guests will enjoy their fine sweets far more than they would a little bottle of cheap wine.

~ Many of today's brides are giving their guests small silver frames as favors. Comparison shop at department stores; for a bulk discount, check with the manager at your local craft store.

FAVORS AND GIFTS SOURCES

Beverly Clark Collection—877-862-3933,
www.beverlyclark.com

Chandler's Candle Company—800-463-7143,
www.chandlerscandle.com

Double T Limited—800-756-6184, www.uniquefavors.com

Exclusively Weddings—800-759-7666,
www.exclusivelyweddings.com

Forever and Always Company—800-404-4025,
www.foreverandalways.com

Gift Emporia.com—www.giftemporia.com

Godiva—800-9-GODIVA, www.godiva.com

Gratitude—800-914-4342, www.giftsofgratitude.com

Personal Creations—800-326-6626

Seasons—800-776-9677

Service Merchandise—800-251-1212,
www.servicemerchandise.com

Tree and Floral Beginnings (seedlings, bulbs, and candles)
800-499-9580, www.plantamemory.com; in Canada,
www.plantamemory.on.ca

Wireless—800-669-9999

Check your local craft supply stores for their selections as well.

∽ Theme wedding favors easily can be made using supplies found at your local craft store, as well. One bride with a beach-themed wedding (held, of course, at the beach) gifted her guests with a small glass bowl (ninety-nine cents each) filled with an inch or two of sand (four dollars for a large bag) and a few seashells and dried starfish (up to ninety-nine cents per piece). So each beach–theme favor cost less than five dollars, and they were beautiful.

∽ Candles are a lovely wedding favor idea, depending on the formality of your wedding. Check gift shops and party supply stores for their selection of pretty, scented candles, and ask for a bulk discount if you will be ordering more than thirty. Note: if you will be placing a large order, do this task a few months ahead of time. Managers will need to place a special order, particularly if the candles you have chosen are handcrafted by a local artist.

34

Wedding Night Accommodations

You'll certainly want to spend your first night together in memorable surroundings. Use this chapter to plan your wedding night accommodations for less.

✐ Get a plain old regular room. Do you really need to pay three times as much for pink walls, nice artwork, a scenic view, and a heart-shaped bed? You'll probably be exhausted after the excitement of the day, and all the facilities and extras may be lost on you. Besides, it's the first night of your honeymoon. You won't be looking at the view or admiring the artwork anyway.

✐ See if you can get your first night's room for free as part of the group discount in the hotel in which your visiting family and friends are staying. One bride negotiated a free weekend stay in the hotel, saving two hundred fifty dollars. Just don't tell your guests which room you're in, or they may find it funny to call you or surprise you.

~ If you have your own place, why not spend the first night there? After all, it's free, and your first night together can make those familiar surroundings new and exciting.

~ Perhaps friends or relatives can let you use their guest cottage. It can be their wedding gift to you.

~ If you'll have to catch a flight at a faraway airport early the next morning, you may choose to spend the night at a hotel near there. Airport-access hotels are often overpriced due to demand, so you'll definitely want to get a no-frills room there. The honeymoon suite will be too costly.

~ However, if you just won't have it any other way—if you *must* have the honeymoon suite—comparison shop around town. You can at least find the lowest price available.

~ The first night spent in a luxury hotel is a great gift idea for parents to consider. They may have wanted to pay for your honeymoon, but they'll be happy you've found them this equally special gesture at less of a blow to their savings. Discuss this idea with them, or with any other relative or friend who might find this an appropriate gift—perhaps the people who introduced you.

35

Planning the Honeymoon

It's the ultimate getaway. Your honeymoon is a vacation to remember, so read on to learn how to get great rates, choose the best honeymoon package for your budget, and avoid extra expenses during your trip.

$\mathcal{W}$here to Begin

∼ Before you start flipping through the travel section of the newspaper or those vacation reviews in the bridal magazines, set your honeymoon budget. A good rule of thumb is to plan on spending a set amount of money you already have available. Don't plan a six-thousand-dollar vacation hoping you'll get at least that much in wedding gift money to cover the cost. If you've estimated wrong, you'll begin married life in debt. So plan on a medium budget (not *too* inexpensive or you'll feel like you've ripped yourself off).

~ Start by searching through Internet travel sites, travel magazines, and brochures to get an idea of where you both would like to spend your honeymoon. Make a wish list that will allow you to compare the pros and cons of each destination.

~ Make a list of what you *don't* want. You may not want a ski vacation or one of those island trips where there's nothing to do all day but lie on the beach. You may be supersensitive to the sun and therefore unwilling to go to the tropics, or you may not want to travel overseas. Before you start your search for your honeymoon spot, it's important that you have some guidelines. The thousands of ideas you come across will be that much easier to narrow down.

~ Check with friends and relatives who travel often or who have just returned from their honeymoon. Where did they go? Would they recommend the same place?

~ Don't fall for travel scams. If you receive a postcard claiming that you've won a cruise, but all you have to do is send ten dollars and your credit card number for verification of your identity, don't do it. You haven't won anything. It's a trick, and the authorities are cracking down on the scam artists who are perpetuating this kind of fraud. So don't believe postcards or mass mailings that sound too good to be true. They are.

The Travel Agent

∾ Use a travel agent. The service is free in most cases, and you're more likely to find out about specials and less expensive packages through a professional who is paid to know these things.

∾ Use your regular travel agent, the one you've booked trips through for years. You can be sure of his or her reliability.

∾ Ask friends and relatives to recommend their travel agent for the job. Again, you'll have evidence of that person's reliability and timeliness.

∾ When looking for your travel agent, consider whether you want the personal service of a smaller agency or the wide-range exposure and knowledge of a larger agency. Both have their pros and cons, so weigh them carefully before you choose.

∼ Make sure the travel agent you choose is a member of the American Society of Travel Agents. Ask for credentials, or check to see the agent's affiliation listed on his or her business card. Check with the Better Business Bureau to see if any charges or complaints have been directed against your agent or the agency.

∼ Does your travel agent seem interested in your wishes, or is he or she just typing codes into the computer with an I-can't-wait-for-lunch attitude? Does she seem knowledgeable? Does he know where to find out such things as a particular destination's climate, code of dress, and customs rules? Does she speak of her own travels? Often, your personal feelings about the travel agent can give you a clue as to whether or not you should be trusting him with these important arrangements.

∼ Go through your company's travel agent. You may get a break if the service is available to you.

∼ You could do all the work yourself, using websites and toll-free numbers to request information. However, this takes up a lot of your time, and some ways to gather prices and times could cost you money. Some major airlines' numbers are listed on page 283.

Choosing a Destination

~ Check with tourist offices for lists of hotels, events, and facilities. You could turn up one of those hidden gems most tourists miss. One bride used this information to find special rates, off-times, and incredible sales and saved one hundred fifty dollars.

~ Check your library's travel books. Volumes of low-cost travel guides have been published, and they're free for the asking. Titles such as *Bermuda on Ten Dollars a Day* can save you a bundle and tip you off to many free attractions.

~ Plan your honeymoon for a place that will be in its off-season. Rates will be lower, special packages will be available, and you'll find fewer crowds and greater bargains everywhere. You can find out about each of your potential destinations' off-season months either in their board of tourism's brochures, on websites, or through your travel agent.

~ Speaking of the season, look at the usual weather patterns of the region you'll be visiting during your honeymoon. Is it going to be hurricane season then? Tornado time? Bad weather can take time away from your vacation, either by keeping you indoors during eight straight days of gale-force winds and rain or by making you miss a few days of your vacation because inclement weather has canceled or delayed your flight there. Again, check in travel brochures or with your agent.

STATE AND LOCATION TOURISM DEPARTMENTS

Tourism Office Worldwide Directory—www.towd.com

Alabama—800-252-2262

Bahamas—800-228-5173

Bermuda—800-223-6107

British Virgin Islands—800-888-5563, ext. 559

Caribbean—212-682-0435

Connecticut—800-282-6863

Delaware—800-441-8846

Disney's Fairy Tale Weddings—407-828-3400

Fiji—310-568-1616

Hawaii—808-923-1811

Jamaica—800-233-4582

Jersey/Cape May County—800-227-2297

Kentucky—800-225-8747

Key West—800-648-6269

Las Vegas—800-426-8695

Lousiana—800-227-4386

Mexico—800-44-MEXICO

Michigan—800-543-2937

Minnesota—800-345-2537

Mississippi—800-647-2290

Montana—800-541-1447

Nebraska—800-228-4307

Nevada—800-638-2328

New Hampshire—800-542-2331

Niagara Falls—800-338-7890

North Carolina—800-847-4862

Oahu, Hawaii—877-525-OAHU, www.visitoahu.com

Oklahoma—800-654-8240

Oregon—800-424-3002

Puerto Rico—800-223-6530

Quebec—800-363-7777

South Carolina—800-872-3505

Tahiti—800-828-6877, www.islandsinthesun.com

U.S. State Department travel advisories—
    www.stolaf.edu/network/travel-advisories.html

Utah—800-222-8824

Virginia—800-248-4833

〜 Pay attention to travel advertisements. Price wars and seasonal specials can reveal great discounts. Just pay attention to the fine print before you call that toll-free number.

~ Look at the international political scene. Is your dream destination currently undergoing some civil unrest that could erupt into full-scale battling? Time spent with five hundred people in a bomb shelter and bullets whistling overhead can put a serious damper on your trip. Check ahead of time by asking your travel agent and by checking international travel magazines that have a danger zone column.

~ Try a non-honeymoon destination. Hotels and resorts specifically geared toward honeymooners are often much higher priced than nonspecialized alternatives. You may be the only honeymooners in the pool, but you won't notice.

~ Don't travel so far away. The farther you go, the more you'll pay. Visit someplace closer to home . . . like a nearby island or a resort town in your state.

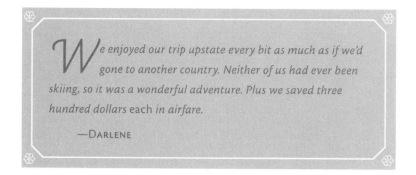

We enjoyed our trip upstate every bit as much as if we'd gone to another country. Neither of us had ever been skiing, so it was a wonderful adventure. Plus we saved three hundred dollars each in airfare.

—DARLENE

AIR-TRAVEL RESOURCES

Airlines

Air Canada—800-776-3000, www.aircanada.ca

America West—800-247-5692, www.americawest.com

American Airlines—800-433-7300, www.amrcorp.com

British Airways—800-247-9297, www.british-airways.com

Continental Airlines—800-525-0280, www.flycontinental.com

Delta Airlines—800-221-1212

KLM Royal Dutch Airlines—800-374-7747

Northwest Airlines—800-225-2525, www.nwa.com

TWA—800-221-2000, www.twa.com

USAir—800-428-4322, www.usair.com

United Airlines—800-241-6522, www.ualservices.com

Virgin Atlantic Airways—800-862-8621

Discount Airfares

Air Fare—www.airfare.com

Cheap Fares—www.cheapfares.com

Cheap Tickets—800-377-1000

Discount Airfare—www.discount-airfare.com

Mr. Cheap—800-MR-CHEAP

Priceline—www.priceline.com

You Price It—www.youpriceit.com

∼ Foreign travel is, of course, much more expensive than a domestic getaway. Distance airfare aside, you're going to have to deal with higher prices in a tourist city and the fluctuating value of the American dollar in foreign currency.

Are Those Honeymoon Packages Worth It?

∼ A hotel's honeymooner's paradise package may turn out to be less of a bargain than it seems. After all, will you really need everything included in the package? Will you want to eat three meals a day in your hotel's restaurant? Will you be playing golf every day? Scuba diving three times in a week? And will you really want to spend your time on a double-decker bus tour with stops at working farms? Take a good look at each element of the package, circle the ones you're sure you'll need, then price only those items separately. You may have to play mathematician, but you could end up with a better price if you're footing the bill just for your room and only the meals and extras you know you'll enjoy.

∼ On the other hand, an all-inclusive package can be a great bargain if your resort or cruise has a lot to offer. Some resorts have several restaurants of varying formality, plus a great variety of activities. One couple reported that their final tab upon checkout was astronomical. They didn't know that each drink they had at the poolside bar cost them twelve dollars! And they had tipped well! Investigate your resort's offerings, estimate how often you plan to venture from the resort, and figure out what the realistic charges might be at the resort. One very resourceful couple called the hotel and asked for copies of the hotel's menus and bar price lists to be faxed to them. They were then able to figure out what the average costs would be, so they wouldn't have to be on a budget during their honeymoon. One look at the price tags for every meal and drink and they jumped at the all-inclusive price.

RESORT RESOURCES

Beaches—800-BEACHES

Club Med—www.clubmed.com

Holiday Inn—www.holiday-inn.com

Radisson—www.radisson.com

Sandals—800-SANDALS, www.sandals.com

Super Clubs—800-GO-SUPER, www.superclubs.com

Swept Away—800-545-7937,
   www.sweptaway.com/weddings.htm

United States Tour Operators Association—800-GO-USTOA,
   www.ustoa.com

⮑ When considering packages, remember to add in the following to the prices: airport arrival and departure taxes, room tax, electricity tax (if applicable), baggage charges, facility fees, cover charges to the nightclub and local attractions, gratuities, service charges for your traveler's checks, transportation rental, and the food and drinks you'll have outside of the meals included in your package.

⮑ Comparison shop among resorts' packages, remembering to look for all the hidden taxes and fees in the small print.

⮑ Investigate the cancellation details. Is any of the deposit nonrefundable?

$\mathcal{B}$ooking Your Room

You will certainly spend a good amount of money here. In fact, you may have been saving money throughout the planning of the wedding just so you and your husband or groom can have top-of-the-line honeymoon accommodations. But you'd still do well to get the best buys you can for your money. This includes protecting your investment with good record keeping and organization.

⮑ The big, fancy hotels with the names known around the world are certainly going to be more expensive than somewhat less flashy ones. Try a three-star hotel instead of a four-star one. You'll hardly notice the difference.

∽ When investigating the larger, more luxurious hotels in the big cities, see if their weekend rates are better than their weekday rates. Most big hotels that cater to weekday business clients will offer Friday-through-Sunday discounts, and these are well worth looking into.

∽ Do you really need the honeymoon suite? Usually, the biggest, most luxurious rooms with the fireplaces and personal swimming pools go for top dollar, so consider the savings of a smaller deluxe room with the necessities. Even the view is negotiable. Of course, this is not to say you should book the dumpiest room they have. You'd be setting yourself up for a huge disappointment when the room doesn't match your fantasies of the perfect honeymoon. Just trim the gaudy extras away. You'll still be in romantic surroundings.

The Honeymoon Flight

∽ Check all the major airlines and comparison shop.

~ Check the price differences between flying on a weekend and flying on a weekday. A ticket for three hundred dollars less might make it worth your while to take a Monday flight.

~ Fly at an off-peak hour. For instance, a discounted midnight flight would be perfect for you if you'd like to get a head start on your honeymoon right from your reception. One bride saved eighty dollars on plane tickets with this option.

~ Keep restrictions in mind when inquiring about low fares. A particular bargain may require you to stay overnight on a Sunday or pay a nonrefundable fee six months before your honeymoon. If you can meet the requirements, no problem. If not, you could be facing a wasted sum of money.

~ Another factor controlling airline prices is the season in which you'll be flying, so keep ticket costs in mind when choosing the date of your wedding and honeymoon. A Christmas weekend wedding may seem like a wonderful idea at first, but it won't be as grand when you're paying three times the normal cost of a ticket and facing holiday rush crowds. Other holiday seasons to look out for: Thanksgiving, New Year's, Easter, spring break, and basically most of the summer. Just do your best to avoid high travel times if you can.

~ See if you'd be better off with a nonstop flight. Direct flights make stops at certain cities along the way to your destination, and the delays could take up your valuable time, especially if you're on a shorter honeymoon. Ask your travel agent if nonstop flights are more or less expensive than other types of flights available to you.

~ On the other hand, some honeymooners see those flights with six-hour layovers to be more of a bargain than a pain in the neck. After all, if your discounted flight has a long break between a change of planes, you've just gotten yourself to a distant major city that you may have enough time to explore a little for just the price of a taxi. Make sure you allow yourself enough time to check in for your next flight, and be back at the airport in time to catch that flight. Margie and Matt spent their layover time in Boston checking out historical landmarks and sharing a cup of clam chowder by the waterfront.

~ You may think that you're getting the best deal possible when you ask for economy tickets, but there may be better deals elsewhere. This is where your travel agent is invaluable. Always ask for the lowest fare available instead of assuming that the so-called economy tickets are the best buy.

~ First-class tickets often cost several times the price of business or coach. What for? A little more leg room? An eight–course meal? Save the difference in expense—you're getting to your destination at the same time as those folks up in the leather seats.

～ Traveling standby may seem like a bargain, but it can be more trouble than it's worth. Do you really want to start off your honeymoon waiting twelve hours in an airport for a cancellation so there's room for you on board?

～ Many brides reported that they flew for free by saving up frequent flier miles earned through business travel or as benefits of certain credit account usage. If you have this option, arrange with your fiancé to save up those points from business and pleasure trips between now and the wedding.

～ Be sure to check the terms of Internet travel discounters carefully. Yes, some sites offer great rates, but you may have to book at the last minute, you may get locked into a higher fare if you book the suggested nine months in advance, and there may be hidden fees. Many brides reported that they saved hundreds of dollars through the use of Internet travel discounters and ticket agents, but they warn others to check all details and make sure the arrangements fit.

～ Look into charter flights. Special arrangements can turn up big savings for you. See what your travel agent knows about these flights.

～ Don't go for ultraspecials without checking them out thoroughly first. Read all the fine print, get your travel agent's advice, then proceed only with a money-back guarantee.

∼ Check cancellation guarantees on all flights you consider. A reputable airline will allow you at least a partial refund in case of emergency or mishap. You may want to consider cancellation insurance. It may cost you a few extra bucks, but your returns in case of a change in plans will reward you.

∼ Get a written copy of your itinerary, including all flight numbers and airline confirmation numbers. On this record of your reservation, record your travel agent's name and the date and time you made your travel arrangements . . . just for assurance.

∼ Get yourself the best bargain possible. See if your student or military ID or AAA card can net you a travel discount.

∼ Ask your travel agent about promotional fares. They, too, may have some travel restrictions, such as time of flight and no frequent flier miles, but they could get you to your honeymoon for a reasonable price.

∼ Ask your travel agent also about fare assurance programs. That way, if a better price comes along for the tickets you purchased at the previous rate, you could be given tickets for the lower fare.

◠ Confirm your flight twenty-four to forty-eight hours in advance. Foreign travel confirmations should be made two to three days in advance.

◠ When you're checking in at the airport, see if you can arrange an upgrade. With some airlines, you can get your seating assignment changed for only thirty or forty dollars. Just be sure to arrive at the airport early, and be prepared to have your request put on standby. This means you'll find out if you've gotten the upgrade at about the same time you're getting on the plane.

Trains and Other Transportation

◠ Compare train travel prices with airline fares. You might find a bargain in a special, and you'll get the wonderful view of a scenic cross-country ride.

TRAIN RESOURCES

Amtrak—800-872-7245, www.amtrak.com

Eurailpass—www.eurail.com

∼ Look for train travel specials in advertisements.

∼ Special train and bus passes can offer you unlimited travel. If you're both adventurers and wouldn't mind a honeymoon-on-the-go, you'll have a pass for an active and scenic honeymoon plus no huge hotel fees—just the two of you together on the road.

∼ If your honeymoon location is close, drive your car. Just make sure it's in working order first, and plan out the most direct and economical route. Again, this is a scenic and adventurous choice. Mandy used her local AAA's services and had them map out the best route for her and her new husband's drive to Colorado. They saved one hundred dollars in gas and lodging with this new plan.

Cruises

∼ Visit your travel agent to collect as much literature as you can on the different cruise lines. Keep in mind the kind of cruise you'd like. An active one? A relaxing one? One with many stops at different islands for sightseeing and souvenir shopping? If you have the kind of cruise you'd like in mind, you'll have a much easier time matching your preferences with the available cruise tours.

CRUISE RESOURCES

A Wedding For You—800-929-4198 (weddings aboard a cruise ship)

American Cruise Line (East Coast from Florida to Maine)—www.americancruiselines.com

American Hawaii Cruises—800-474-9934 (weddings aboard a cruise ship)

Carnival Cruise Lines—www.carnival.com

Cruise Lines International Association—www.cruising.org

Cunard—www.cunardline.com

Discount Cruises—www.cruise.com

Disney Cruises—www.disneycruise.com

Holland America—www.hollandamerica.com

Norwegian Cruise Lines—800-262-4NCL, www.ncl.com

Princess Cruises—www.princess.com

Radisson 7 Sevens Cruises—www.rssc.com

Royal Caribbean—800-727-2717, www.royalcaribbean.com

For further comparison shopping, go on-line and check out Person-alogic at *www.personalogic.com* for detailed information on a variety of destinations. The in-depth reviews of each cruise line's offerings mention price lists for grade of room, ratings, dress code, cuisine style, surcharges, tipping, amenities such as pools and saunas, and the type *of clientele—couples, families, singles, or seniors. Yes, these reviews are subjective, but the information is there for your comparison shopping.*

⌁ Ask your family and friends who cruise often to recommend their favorite ships and tours.

⌁ The location of your cabin can affect the price of your tickets. Top-deck, outside, and center-of-the-boat cabins are more expensive than their opposites, and most cruise goers claim that a room on the waterline provides a much more stable ride. Look at the positioning of the rooms on those color-coded boat charts you'll find in most cruise brochures, and pay special attention to the square footage of the rooms you're considering.

Out-of-the-Ordinary Honeymoon Destinations

⌁ For all of the romance and quiet seclusion and none of the honeymoon industry's expensive extras, try a getaway at a bed-and-breakfast. Check your library for a free guidebook of the best, or surf the Internet for great ideas and leads.

⌒ Camping is a romantic way to spend your honeymoon . . . alone together in the middle of nature with the moon and stars above. It may not be a week at a four-star hotel, but it's still a great vacation for less of a dent in your budget. A hint: make sure you're not planning this camping trip during your region's rainy season. Getting stuck in your tent all week may sound romantic, but you still have to take into account the cold, the mud, the after-rain mosquitoes. . . . For information on camping locations and regulations, write to:

National Park Service
U.S. Dept. of the Interior
18th & C Streets, NW
Washington, DC 20240

⌒ Try a canoeing or sailing adventure honeymoon. All you need to do is set out with your own or borrowed equipment with a map and plenty of instruction, and you're set for a wild and memorable ride.

⌒ Try the ocean, lakes, mountains, and cities near you. Some of the best-kept secrets are hidden much closer to home than you think.

Your Honeymoon Preparations

~ Apply for your passport way in advance. Don't leave the job for the last minute—passports take several weeks, if not months, to process. Don't be one of those unorganized brides who doesn't get her passport in time for the European honeymoon and then has to cancel the trip with no refund. How painful.

~ Prepare your luggage for the trip by making sure your luggage tags have your correct name and address on them. Pack a sheet of paper stating your name and honeymoon destination inside your suitcases just in case they get misdirected.

~ Don't overpack. A too-heavy case could wind up costing you extra. Most airlines have weight restrictions, and their extra fees aren't minor.

~ Try to pack everything you'll need for your honeymoon. Having to buy lotion or toothpaste at your hotel's gift shop could cost you a lot of money. Items stocked there are overpriced, particularly film for your camera. So pack well.

CARRY-ON ITEMS

Tickets	Hotel's name and
Passports	address
Copy of your	Eyeglasses or
marriage license	contact lenses
Traveler's checks	Lens-cleaning solution
Credit cards	Contraception
Itinerary with contact	Prescription
phone numbers	medications
Hotel confirmation	Camera and film
information	Addresses for postcards
Car rental confirmation	Extra clothes in case
information	of a layover
Good jewelry	

〜 Set up a house sitter to watch your home and possessions and feed your pets while you're away. Give the house sitter a list of important phone numbers and instructions (such as trash day and directions to local stores), and leave explicit rules about parties, guests, and access to your food. A non–live-in could simply take in your mail and newspapers, feed and walk the dog, and park the car in your driveway to give the appearance that someone is home. When the visiting caretaker is away, continue the illusion with timed lights and a timed stereo.

Automatic sensor lights that come on when motion is detected by the doors or windows are another break-in deterrent.

Save Money on Your Honeymoon

~ Eat some casual meals during your honeymoon. If you take every meal in the hotel's dress-up dining room, you'll pay much more than if you had grabbed a sandwich and fries at the pool bar for lunch a few times. Besides, then you won't have to miss a moment in the sun by going in, showering, and dressing for a meal.

~ Don't drink too much alcohol. At least not at every meal and at every trip to the poolside bar. As you know, alcoholic drinks are much more expensive than the nonalcoholic kinds—especially when you add on the resort's already higher price tags. A frozen daiquiri at a Caribbean bar last summer cost one bride eleven dollars. And it was served in a plastic cup! Be prepared for high prices at the beverage and food concessions.

~ Room service means an extra charge just for the waiter to walk up to your room. Why not carry a bottle of champagne and a fruit platter upstairs yourself, or sneak down and pick up something to surprise your husband while he's running a bubble bath for you?

∼ Get a room with a refrigerator and a stove so that you can prepare some simpler snacks and drinks. Go to a nearby market in town and stock up on sodas and fruit and keep those in your refrigerator.

∼ Stay clear of those little stocked refrigerators that seem to offer you every kind of drink and snack under the sun. You will be overcharged for each of those items.

∼ Your membership in a professional organization could lead to discounts for you if you ask for them. Talk to your organization's headquarters.

∼ If you're in a foreign country, don't exchange your money at the street vendor's stand, in airports and train stations, or at tourist attractions. You'll get better rates and therefore more for your dollar when you change your money at reputable banks.

∼ Pay careful attention to the customs regulations of the area. Make sure your souvenirs can be legally brought home and that you haven't purchased more than you can take home duty-free. You will have to pay customs on anything over a certain price.

~ Be careful about using your credit card when you're buying items or services overseas. You may wind up paying the dollar rate at the time of billing rather than at the time of purchase. Then again, if the dollar has fallen into a slump since then, you're actually getting that great buy for much less of a bargain. And your credit card company *can* offer you some security in your purchases by investigating trouble and possibly reimbursing you for lost or stolen merchandise.

~ One of the simplest and fastest ways to get cash overseas is at an ATM (cash machine). Just follow the instructions (generally available in English as well as the local language). Most machines will accept either your cash station card or a major credit card (just like in the States).

~ Use traveler's checks that can be used at face value and don't charge a service fee.

~ Use your auto club's regular discounts.

~ Don't rent a car at the airport. Rental agencies there may be overpriced.

～ Is it less expensive to rent a car for a week than for four days? Look into the agency's pricing structure and do some creative figuring.

～ Reserve your car ahead of time so you're not left renting a van at extra cost because it's all they have.

～ Keep track of the car's mileage. You'll want to make sure you're charged the correct amount. Being on your honeymoon won't protect you from getting ripped off. You'll have to protect yourselves.

RESOURCES FOR RENTAL CAR COMPANIES

Alamo—800-327-9633, www.goalamo.com

Avis—800-831-2847, www.avis.com

Dollar—800-800-4000, www.dollar.com

Econocar—888-326-6697, www.econocar-baweb.com

Enterprise—800-325-8007, www.enterprise.com

Hertz—800-654-3131, www.hertz.com

Check your Yellow Pages for other companies near you.

Note: Be sure to check with the rental companies you call about their restrictions and age requirements. Some companies will not rent cars or other vehicles to persons under twenty-five years of age. Find this out before you reserve your car.

〜 Plan all your car travel for one or two days so that you're getting the most for a shorter rental time. It doesn't make sense to rent the car for a week and only use it two or three days.

〜 Rent bikes or scooters instead. Comparison shop around your honeymoon spot for the best rates, or ask the hotel's social guide to help you track down the best prices.

〜 Get bus and train passes so you won't have to take expensive taxis around town. There's no better way to absorb the local flavor. One married couple figured their train transport saved them ninety-five dollars in taxi fares.

〜 Many big-city theaters sell same-day performance tickets at discounted prices. If you're a smart shopper, you could wind up with prime seats at lower than low prices.

〜 Look for free tours and attractions in your guidebooks. They will have every bit as much local flavor as those that charge for admittance.

〜 Buy small, inexpensive souvenirs. Remember the luggage weight requirements? You'll have to meet those on the way home, too. Or take home free souvenirs: coasters, bar napkins, brochures, shells, rocks, even some sand or ocean water in a small bottle.

36

Your Trousseau

While you're having fun on your honeymoon you might as well look your best. You could max out your credit cards to buy new vacation outfits and accessories, but this is not a fashion show. Many brides have shared their trousseau secrets with me; after seeing their honeymoon photos I couldn't agree more that they made the economically correct clothing decisions. This chapter will help you decide on the right purchases for your trip, so you can have something new without an expense that you'll be paying off forever.

⌁ You don't have to buy a whole new wardrobe. That may have been the case in the old days, but now it's smarter to just buy a few special new pieces and fill in the gaps with your favorite vacation clothes and shoes.

～ Buy clothing you can use again. Onetime wearings aren't worth the ticket price.

～ Stay away from top-name, high-priced clothing stores. Why get one item for two hundred dollars when you can get five great new things for the same price elsewhere?

～ Don't shop in bridal boutiques for your honeymoon outfits and lingerie. Go to regular department stores and mid-priced lingerie boutiques instead for better choices and better prices.

～ Shop at discount stores and in outlets for incredible bargains in your area.

～ Don't overbuy, using your honeymoon as an excuse to splurge on yourself. Of course, the temptation will be there, but act in moderation. Consider the money you save to be money in your airfare fund.

～ If you have shoes that are in good condition and are suitable for your vacation, use them. Besides the money you save, you're also saving the pain and trouble of breaking in new shoes on a tour. There's no time for blisters on a honeymoon.

∼ Don't shop for your trousseau until after your bridal showers. You just may get all the lingerie and robes you'll ever need as gifts. One bride originally budgeted two hundred dollars for her honeymoon lingerie. After receiving a roomful of teddies and bustiers, she redirected that money to her attendants' gifts. Overall, she saved two hundred dollars.

∼ Pamper yourself with new lingerie and undergarments more than with outer clothing. A trousseau fund spent entirely on teddies and garters will make for a more interesting trip than new shorts and earrings.

Your Going-Away Outfit

∼ Instead of buying a brand-new, expensive dress specifically for the trip from the reception to the airport (or from the reception to the hotel), use one of your honeymoon dresses.

∼ Perhaps your going-away dress can be a gift from your mother or grandmother.

∼ Or just make your grand exit from the reception in your wedding gown, then change at home into casual clothes for more comfortable traveling to the airport or hotel. You won't even need a going-away outfit.

37

Guest Lodging

If you have guests coming in from out of town you might choose to pay for their lodging expenses. Learn how to find suitable accommodations for them with your budget in mind, plus treat them a little with the savings you've found.

◦ Comparison shop for the best-priced hotels in town, taking care not to book a dive just because of its low prices. A room in a cockroach-infested truck stop is no way to welcome your favorite people. So look around, ask to see the rooms, and talk to people who are actually staying at the hotel.

◦ A good idea is to book the rooms in the hotel where the reception is being held. That way, no one has to get in a car and drive after the party. You may even get a special discount.

HOTEL RESOURCES

All Hotels—www.all-hotels.com

Bed-and-breakfasts, country inns, and small hotels—
www.virtualcities.com/ons/Oonsadex.htm

Bed-and-breakfast—international guide—www.ibbp.com

Cyber Rentals—www.opendoor.com/rentals/homepage.html

Fodors—www.fodors.com

Go Native's Guide to Bed and Breakfast Inns—
www.go-native.com

Hilton—www.hilton.com

Hotel Anywhere—www.earthlink.net/~hotelanywhere

National Park Service—www.nps.gov

Radisson—www.radisson.com

Travelocity—www.travelocity.com

∽ Ask about group rates. If you're planning to book a certain number of rooms, you'll undoubtedly get a break. Jo estimated her savings at twenty-five dollars per room.

∽ Plan for your guests to share their rooms, if they'll agree to it. Besides being a savings to you, it can actually be fun for them. No doubt they'll all have their doors open and be wandering around the halls as if the building were a college dorm.

∼ Don't let these guests come into town too early. Two days ahead of time is more than enough. You don't want to have to entertain them while there's so much for you to do, and unnecessary days' accommodations just rack up extra hotel bills. Make it clear that everyone is to arrive only a day or two before the wedding.

∼ If there aren't too many people coming in from out of town, consider putting them up at your place, at relatives' homes, and at kind neighbors' houses. Again, besides the obvious savings, it's a fun change of pace to be able to spend time with a houseguest.

∼ Place inexpensive gifts in your guests' rooms. Good ideas are baskets of soft drinks and snacks, maps and listings of interesting things to see and do in the area, and toys and games for the kids. Always include a personal note, thanking your guests for coming to town.

38

The Rehearsal Dinner

Here's where it all starts to come together. The plans are set and it's walk-through time. After the rehearsal, once everyone gets their places and lines in order, you'll head off for your last party as engaged people. The rehearsal dinner is a festive event with everyone sharing in the excitement, proposing toasts, and looking forward to the next day. You can help plan a memorable dinner on any budget. Here are some ideas for you to consider.

~ Your informal rehearsal dinner could be a pizza party, a barbecue in the yard, a pool party, or even a trip to the beach.

~ You can still have a sit-down dinner. Just serve it at home instead of at a fancy restaurant. Choose from inexpensive meals that stretch to feed a crowd: pasta, stew, Mexican fare, home-made pizzas set up in a make-your-own arrangement.

∼ Plan the menu carefully. Offer a choice of two or three preselected, reasonably priced menu items rather than allowing guests to order whatever they'd like off the menu. That keeps lobster off the tab.

∼ Preselect wine and beverage items, as well, rather than allowing guests to order pricey drinks and shots. If you're holding an informal rehearsal dinner, pitchers of beer and soda are fine in addition to moderately priced bottles of wine.

∼ There's no need for a specially made cake at the rehearsal dinner. That's for tomorrow. Instead, plan to offer an inexpensive dessert for your rehearsal dinner guests.

∼ Have dessert and coffee at a nice café. The term *rehearsal dinner* doesn't *have* to mean dinner.

∼ Skip the professional photographer. While you'll undoubtedly want some record of this gathering, it's enough to take your own shots or get copies of those taken by your family and friends. There's no need to spend five hundred dollars for a professional photo session of the rehearsal dinner.

39

Your Personal Beauty Care

The bride deserves the royal treatment on her wedding day. It's possible to get all the pampering and primping you need while still respecting your budget. Learn how to create a gorgeous wedding day look at little cost.

〜 Don't buy all new makeup just for your wedding. You're better off using your makeup for the more natural look you're used to. Some less frugal brides have reported dropping one hundred twenty-five dollars on glamour-line cosmetics. The rest of us could find a better use for that money.

〜 If you must buy new makeup, don't go for the disgustingly overpriced kinds. Comparison shop for bargains, or see if you can find the same brand and color you normally use.

∽ Scout out the makeup counters for free samples. Just one of those little tubes of lipstick is enough to keep you in the pink throughout your wedding day. Just don't attempt to grab fourteen of those little samples. There's a difference between making good use of a sample and taking advantage.

∽ Get samples for each bridesmaid to use. They can grab their own when they're out shopping with you, and they've saved ten to twenty dollars as well.

∽ All of your bridesmaids and honor attendants can use the same bottle of nail polish. No need for each to buy her own.

∽ Do your own makeup. After all, you'll do the most natural-looking job on yourself. A professional might overpaint you . . . and then expect to be paid for the stuff you'll just wipe off later anyway. Besides, some brides find it relaxing to do their own makeup on their wedding day. Just give yourself plenty of time.

COMPARE AND SAVE

Professional makeup application . . . . $30–$50

Do it yourself . . . . free

⌒ Don't attempt to give yourself a home perm if you've never done one before. This is no time to take chances with your hair just to save a few bucks. Instead, go to your trusted beautician. Your hair is worth the money.

⌒ If you've always dyed your hair and you're comfortable with the way it turns out every time, then there's no reason you shouldn't do your own touch-ups rather than go to a salon.

COMPARE AND SAVE

Salon dye job .... $50–$100

At-home dye job .... $5–$15

⌒ Few brides would take the chance of cutting their own hair just for the money saved. A good haircut is the basis of the bride's style, and it's also an inexpensive way to get that pampered feeling without the full line of extravagances. So the best way to watch your finances when it comes to haircuts is simply to stay with your regular stylist. A too-cheap salon you've found on a back road may give terrible, disastrous haircuts, and a gaudy, overpriced one will give you a standard chop with an outrageous bill attached. The best way to save money on your haircut: just have a wash and cut instead of the wash, cut, and style.

⌇ Have a bridesmaid or even a neighbor French braid your hair for you if you like the look but can't do it yourself. The favor saves you salon prices, which can run up to fifty dollars for this simple service.

⌇ Have a bridesmaid pin your headpiece on for you. Why would you need to go to a salon for that and then have to drive home with your headpiece on?

⌇ Use your own home waxing kit rather than go to a salon. Again, savings can reach anywhere from fifteen to more than one hundred dollars.

⌇ If you insist on a tan, worship the sun instead of a tanning booth. Just be smart about sunblock and avoid direct sun and UV times—11 A.M. to 3 P.M.

⌇ Do your own nails. And if you like the look of a French manicure, practice on yourself using a French manicure kit.

> **COMPARE AND SAVE**
>
> Salon nails .... $20–$50
>
> Home job .... free

⮑ Advise your maids to do their makeup, waxing, tanning, and manicures for themselves as well. They'll save money, and you won't wind up with any cosmetic nightmares walking down the aisle ahead of you.

As cost effective as these tips are, you may still find it worth the expense to go for the royal treatment at your beauty salon. In fact, many brides and their bridal parties say the morning spent at the salon enjoying the full bridal package did much to ease their nerves and make them feel more beautiful than if they had done the jobs themselves. They wouldn't trade the experience. Of course there's nothing wrong with that. Your salon may offer you their wedding morning package at a price that's right for you.

⮑ You can enjoy the salon treatment for less than the bridal package deal, though. Do you all need facials? It may not be a good idea to have one right before the wedding, in case of irritation. Do you all need pedicures? Massages? Color analysis?

Espresso and continental breakfast? Make a deal with the salon owner instead for you to get a group rate for hair stylings and—if you choose—manicures. The package deal you work out for yourself will undoubtedly be much less expensive. One bride negotiated her bridal beauty package down fifty dollars. You could do the same.

∽ Prepare an emergency kit with clear nail polish, a small sewing kit, aspirin, a nail file, club soda, extra lipstick and face powder, and even a stapler for last-minute mishaps and touch-ups. Have someone keep it in his or her car or take it to the reception.

40

Gifts for Others

Your loved ones have given you a gift by attending your wedding, helping you plan it, or helping pay for it. Show them how much you appreciate those actions with a gift they'll cherish forever. You can spend a fortune on your selections, but the meaning counts more than the price. Read on for some ideas on how to choose the perfect gift for everyone on your list.

~ Don't buy the fancy thank-you gifts sold in bridal salons and bridal catalogs. By now you know you can do much better than that.

~ Look for sales in local stores, in newspaper and magazine advertisements, even in regular gift catalogs.

~ Buy many of the same items (such as frames or gold pens) and negotiate a discount for the group purchase.

INEXPENSIVE GIFT IDEAS

For the Women

sachets	frames
jewelry	photo albums
chocolates	candles
aromatherapy	lockets
products	clocks

For the Men

wallets	key chains
gold pen sets	photo albums
beer mugs	cuff links
scarves	clocks
frames	

For the Children

jewelry for the	stuffed animals
ceremony	and toys

~ Consider gift certificates for makeovers, golf games, lingerie, CDs, even home repair and babysitting services. These, of course, will not be kept forever, but they'll certainly be appreciated as thoughtful gifts. Plus they can be found at low prices—some for *no* prices.

∾ Speaking of gifts, do you have insurance for your wedding gifts? The expense is worth it.

∾ Arrange for someone, perhaps your parents, to take your wedding gifts to your home or to theirs after the reception for safekeeping while you're away. This is one of the best forms of insurance known. Never leave your house empty *and* full of new and valuable merchandise.

∾ Have baskets filled with midnight munchies delivered to their hotel rooms after the reception. You can make all the cookies, brownies, and candies yourself and have a friend make the delivery after you've left for your honeymoon. More rowdy bridal parties who are planning to continue the celebration long into the night will appreciate your sending over several bottles of champagne . . . or the leftovers from the reception!

∾ Not to be dismissed is the handwritten thank-you note. A personal letter is always treasured and is priceless.

41

Parties and More Parties!

From the bachelorette party to the wedding morning brunch, there will be plenty of opportunities to celebrate with your favorite people. To avoid overspending on these fun occasions, keep the following hints in mind as you plan.

The Bridal Luncheons

⁓ An informal brunch or luncheon is always a good alternative to the fancier, more expensive bridal soirees. Instead of having it at a restaurant, hold the luncheon at your home. Most brides who opt for this kind of get-together can expect to save up to one hundred dollars, depending on the number of guests and the menu.

~ If you'll be hosting the party at home, prepare light foods, appetizers, or an inexpensive entrée that can feed a group. Or just have dessert.

~ Or you could skip the whole luncheon idea and opt instead for a shower or rehearsal dinner to take its place.

The Bachelorette Party

~ Make this celebration an informal affair. You can all go out to a local tavern or restaurant and share the bill. Your bridesmaids may even pick up the tab for you if they choose.

~ Hold the party at home or at a bridesmaid's house as an economical move.

~ For a night on the town, provide the responsible services of a designated driver. Instead of the costly limousine, have a nondrinker volunteer for the job. Or you could go by the current trend and not drink that night.

~ Another alternative for an even better time: join forces with the men and make it a coed party. If all agree, combine the bachelor party with the bachelorette party, and all of you can go out dancing. Besides, no one's left to wonder what the other is up to.

∼ Or don't have a bachelorette party at all. Your shower or rehearsal dinner may take its place as just a fun night out with your family and friends.

The Wedding Day Bridal Brunch

∼ Don't have it catered. While it's good to have some light food available so you and your bridal party and family can get something in your stomachs, there's no need to call in the catering trucks with the big silver trays of quiche and finger sandwiches. Either buy a bag of frozen bagels or a few boxes of rolls and add the fixin's, or plan to cook up some quick light food. No one's going to want to eat very much that morning anyway.

∼ Skip the champagne toast or mimosas. Drink juice, water, or coffee to get you going. Some brides reported that starting their wedding morning with champagne or wine on an empty, nervous stomach caused them to feel sick, tired, or headachy later in the day.

∽ Curb the wedding morning guest list. Some parents of the bride and groom have been known to invite grandparents and aunts and uncles for the bridal breakfast, which adds to the brunch expenses. It also means a more crowded, chaotic home and fewer people who see you in your gown for the first time as you're walking down the aisle.

∽ Skip the wedding morning brunch if your beauty salon visit will include a continental breakfast for you and your bridal party. Call the salon and ask if that's a part of their bridal offerings or a regular part of their services, and plan to have your breakfast during your pedicure. Be careful of price: some salons charge for this breakfast service and you can provide a lovely brunch for less per person at home after the hair and nails are done.

∽ Send some food over to where the groom and his men are getting ready for the ceremony. They have to eat, too. Your brother, the usher, can take some with him when he goes over.

Author's Note

Of course, there are many more ways to save money on your wedding than the ideas mentioned here. You may have near you a fabulous source of materials or flowers, and you may live in a region that offers more moderate prices for wedding services than those of other areas. Yet, although this book cannot give you dates and addresses of the best buys near you, it has taught you to spend your money with quality in mind. It has shown you how to protect your investments and to keep organized.

You've become a smarter wedding shopper, and I don't doubt that you'll save plenty of money on your pre-wedding activities, wedding, reception, and honeymoon. All without the savings showing.

Best of luck on your wedding and in your new life together!

Index